Spring Woodland Flowers of Illinois

Solomon's Seal
(Polygonatum biflorum)

STEVE CHADDE

Spring Woodland Flowers of Illinois

Steve Chadde

AN ORCHARD INNOVATIONS FIELD GUIDE
ISBN 978-1951682569

Illustrations are from the author's collection, public domain sources, and photographs made available for commercial use under Creative Commons license Attribution 4.0 International (CC BY 4.0). The author gratefully acknowledges these photographers who have shared their images of the natural world.

COVER IMAGES
Front cover: *Geranium maculatum* (top), *Erythronium americanum* (lower left), *Sanguinaria canadensis* (lower center), *Silene virginica* (lower right).
Back cover: *Claytonia virginica.*

The Biota of North America Program (*www.bonap.org*) provided permission to use their data to generate the distribution maps.

The author can be contacted by email: *steve@chadde.net*
VER. 1.0 01/2022

CONTENTS

PREFACE

Spring Woodland Wildflowers of Illinois is an introduction to the early flowering plants found in the woods and forests of Illinois. It is intended for the person wanting to learn more about the state's wildflowers, and the 112 plants species covered are those one will most commonly see during hikes through Illinois forests in the spring.

Much of the text is based on a work of the same title published in 1980 by the Illinois Department of Conservation, and authored by Robert H. Mohlenbrock, Department of Botany, Southern Illinois University. The work is made available under a Creative Commons Attribution 4.0 license (CC BY 4.0). For more information see: *creativecommons.org/licenses/by/4.0/*

In this new edition, additional information has been added, scientific names and family assignments have been updated (based primarily on ITIS, the Integrated Taxonomic Information System, *www.itis.gov*), county-level distribution maps added based on data provided by BONAP (the Biota of North America Program, *www.bonap.org*), and all new color photographs prepared.

The result is a field guide that will help anyone interested in the state's wildflowers to become more proficient in both naming and also understanding the rich flora found in Illinois forests.

INTRODUCTION

Wildflowers hold a special fascination for many people in all walks of life and at all ages. There is excitement in seeing the first wildflower in the spring after a long, cold winter. There is a thrill in watching the forests and prairies and roadsides burst into flower as the seasons progress. While some may be satisfied with simply admiring the natural beauty of wildflowers, others have a desire to know the names of these flowers. Unfortunately, introductory identification guides to wildflowers are scarce. Technical floras are available for the serious student, but these generally employ an extensive scientific terminology, and are rarely illustrated in color.

This book is an introduction on the identification of the more common woodland wildflowers found in Illinois, and which bloom from February until the end of May. Included are descriptions, photographs, and distribution maps for 112 of these plant species. Of course, since there are nearly 3,400 species of flowering plants in Illinois, many more plants are present in the woodlands of Illinois. However, this book will help you identify the ones you are most likely to encounter in the spring before the leafy canopy of trees limits their growth and flowering.

Scope

A plant may be included in this book if (a) its primary habitat is a woodland or forest, (b) if it flowers primarily by the end of May, and (c) if it is an herbaceous (non-woody) plant.

A woodland is simply defined as a habitat which is dominated by trees. The woodland may be dry, rich and shaded, or low and wet. It is not possible to draw a line after the last day in May as a cut-off for spring-flowering plants because all plants have a range of flowering time. In addition, plants which flower at a given time in the southern part of Illinois bloom several days later in the northern part of Illinois. In general, plants which bloom in southern Illinois in May but which do not begin to flower in northern Illinois until June are excluded from this book. Some plants which bloom in Illinois during May may continue to bloom throughout the summer; they generally are included.

Only herbaceous plants are included in this book — trees, shrubs, and vines are excluded. Grasses and sedges, apart from one grass (*Poa sylvestris*) and one grass-like species (*Luzula multiflora*), although flowering plants, are excluded because of their usually non-showy flowers and their difficulty in identification. Plants of prairies, roadsides, exposed bluff-tops, and standing water are excluded unless they occur in woodland habitats as well. Weedy, non-native plants whose origin is in Europe or Asia or South America are also excluded.

Many of the plants included are known from most parts of Illinois, although they may be more common in one area than in another. A few are limited to the southern area of Illinois, while others are only in northern Illinois. The state map for each species indicates known presence or absence from a particular county, based on verified collection records.

Format

The book is divided first on the basis of flower color. The color groupings are **red and pink, orange and yellow, blue and purple** (including lavender, violet, and maroon), **white**, and **green**. In addition, a small group of plants with unusual flower structure or a peculiar color is included within the green flower section. Within each color group, the flowers are arranged alphabetically by the scientific name of the family. This arrangement generally groups flowers of similar structure together. Accompanying each description are one or more photographs of the features of the plant. In addition to the description for each species, there are statements concerning habitat, time of flowering, uses, and the origin of each plant's generic name.

Only a few technical terms have been used, most of which are described below, and a **glossary** is included on page 125.

PLANT STRUCTURES

Root

The root of a plant functions as an anchorage as well as an organ of absorption and food storage. Plants with roots lasting but one season are called **annuals** and propagate themselves solely by seeds. Those forms with roots lasting two years are known as **biennials**. During the first year the root establishes itself by storing food and water, and later in that season gives rise to a short stem with a cluster of basal leaves. During the following year the plant completes its development and then dies after setting fruit and seeds. Like an annual, it too reproduces itself by seeds. The **perennial** plant is one in which the rootstock or underground stem persists year after year and, in this way, sustains the species. Perennials also can propagate themselves by seeds.

Roots may be classified as **fibrous** when they are made up of numerous main roots coming from a common point, as in most grasses, or **tap** if there is one main root, often fleshy, with many lateral roots (as in the cultivated carrot).

Stem

The axial portion of a plant connecting the root with the aerial parts (foliage) is called the **stem** and is distinguished from the roots by having joints (nodes). Leaf buds and lateral shoots develop at the nodes. The spaces between two nodes are called **internodes**. Most stems are held aboveground but some types are found growing horizontal to the ground or completely subterranean. One of these specialized stems is called a **bulb** which is made up of a very short stalk surrounded by many fleshy leaves. Onions and lilies represent this type. A **corm** is another underground stem somewhat similar to the above but lacking the fleshy leaves. This stem is dorsally flattened with nodes close together bearing dry scaly leaves, an example is the garden gladiolus. A **rhizome** is an elongated underground stem with nodes compressed together and is present in Iris. A fleshy underground stem with nodes appearing as "eyes" is called a **tuber**; the potato is a good example of this type of stem.

Stems are considered **simple** when made up of one main axis or branching when lateral shoots occur. Although most stems are vertical (erect), some are oblique or somewhat parallel to the ground and referred to as **spreading**. When stems are flat on the ground they are termed **prostrate**.

Leaves

Leaves are lateral outgrowths of stem tips and are responsible for the food-making process (photosynthesis) in plants. Many leaves are divided into a flat surface called the **blade** and a narrow stalk, the **petiole**. In leaves of this type the blade is often referred to as the leaf and measured as such with another dimension given for the petiole. Leaves lacking a petiole, with the blades flush with the stem, are termed **sessile**. Others which completely surround the stem are called **perfoliate**. Some leaves have small accessory leaves below where they join the stem and these are called **stipules**.

Two leaves opposite each other at a node have an **opposite** arrangement or, if more than two, **whorled**, while others are arranged **alternately**. Leaves clustered close to the ground are termed **basal** or, if in a tight circular clump, a **rosette**.

Leaves are classified as **simple** or **compound**. A compound leaf is one in which the blade has been divided into definite separate units (**leaflets**), these often being mistaken for leaves. Sometimes simple leaves are deeply lobed, appearing like compound leaves. These variations can lead to errors in identification. A leaf is generally subtended by a bud at the point where it joins the stem.

Flowers

Flowers generally are made up of four parts: **sepals**, **petals**, **stamens** and **pistils** (carpels). These are joined on a base called the **receptacle**. The stalk of an individual flower is a **pedicel** or **peduncle** but the latter term is more correctly used in referring to the stalk of a flower cluster (**inflorescence**) or a single flower with the stalk rising from the ground or a cluster of basal leaves.

Sepals are collectively referred to as the **calyx**, while the collection of petals is the **corolla**. Both structures are included within the term **perianth**. Petals may occur separately, or fused, or be lacking.

The corolla may be **regular** with all the petals equal; or **irregular**, with petals unequal and sometimes modified into spurs, hoods, or other appendages. Examples of regular flowers are rose, poppy, buttercup; irregular flowers include larkspur, violet, orchid, clover, most species of Penstemon and members of the Mint family (Lamiaceae). Irregular flowers are often 2-lipped, and classified as strongly 2-lipped if one lip noticeably exceeds the other in length, or slightly 2-lipped if the difference is not very apparent.

Stamens usually consist of a narrow stalk called the **filament** and the pollen-producing portion, the **anther**. In some flowers the filaments are fused into a tube surrounding the pistil, while in most the filaments are separate. At times the anthers are found fused together. Flowers with stamens only are termed **staminate**.

The pistil or carpel is made up of a pollen-collecting tip, the **stigma**, a slender **style** (not always present) and the **ovary** which may have one compartment (1-celled) or several. Flowers with their calyxes tightly fused about the ovary and with the other structures inserted above it are designated as having an **inferior ovary** (epigynous). Those with the calyxes not fused as above and with the stamens and petals inserted below the ovary, have a **superior ovary** (hypogynous). In some instances flower parts are borne on the rim of a concave receptacle which places them above or below the ovary depending on the curve of the receptacle. This is called a **transitional ovary** (perigynous). Flowers bearing pistils but no stamens are known as **pistillate flowers**.

The arrangement of a flower or flowers on a stalk (peduncle) is called an **inflorescence**. In the Aster family (Asteraceae) the inflorescence is made up of many flowers on a flat or convex receptacle surrounded by bracts which are collectively referred to as the **involucre**. This type of flower cluster is called a head and may possess different kinds of flowers. Some heads are composed wholly of strap-shaped flowers (**ray flowers**) as in the dandelion. Others have tubular flowers (**disc flowers**) only, as in thistles. A third type of arrangement is made up of tubular flowers in the center and ray flowers on the outside as in the common sunflower. It is called the **radiate type**. In this same family, the calyx of certain flowers is often modified into scale or feather-like appendages called **pappus**. Some of these structures are also present on the receptacle between the flowers.

Fruits

A fruit is technically a ripened ovary which may assume a number of forms. A **legume** is a 1-compartmented fruit splitting along two sides as in the garden pea and lupine. A similar type fruit which splits only along one side is a **follicle** and best seen in milkweed plants. A **capsule** is made up of two or more compartments and splits along a number of lines of weakness. Jimson Weed and Iris possess this type of fruit.

A fleshy fruit containing one seed with a stony covering (the inner part of the ovary wall) is termed a **drupe** as seen in cherry. Fleshy fruits with one or several seeds, lacking the stony covering, are called **berries** and are exemplified by gooseberries and grapes. A single-compartmented fruit in which the seed coat is tightly fused with the ovary wall is called a **grain** (caryopsis) as in cultivated corn. A similar type with the seed coat and the ovary wall not fused is called an **achene** and is seen in sunflower fruits. Classifications of other types of fruits can be found in most botany texts.

Seeds

The plant ovary contains one or several small units called **ovules** which mature into **seeds**. The surfaces of seeds vary in texture and some seeds have accessory structures like wings. These characteristics are important in the positive identification of certain plant species.

NATURAL DIVISIONS OF ILLINOIS

Illinois has a diversity of landscapes that can be described by differences in topography, glacial history, bedrock, soils, and the distribution of native plants and animals. Using these natural features, Illinois has been divided into 14 natural divisions, briefly described below (and see map, page 11). The natural divisions of Illinois were defined in 1973 in a technical report authored by then state botanist John Schwegman and colleagues. According to Schwegman, "Natural divisions are geographic regions of a larger entity like a state or a continent. A division contains similar landscapes, climates, and substrate features like bedrock and soils that support similar vegetation and wildlife over the division's area."

The natural divisions have been further subdivied into 33 subdivisions. For further information, see the website of the Illinois Natural History Survey: *www.inhs.illinois.edu/outreach/natural-divisions/*

1. The **Wisconsin Driftless Natural Division** is part of an area extending from the northwestern corner of Illinois into Iowa, Wisconsin, and Minnesota that escaped Pleistocene glaciation. Historically, most of this division was covered in hardwood forest, and uniques features such as dolomite outcrops and caves.

2. The **Rock River Hill Country Natural Division** of north-central and northwestern Illinois is a region of rolling, glaciated topography drained by the Rock River. Historically, prairie occupied large expanses of level uplands, with forests and woodlands along waterways.

3. The **Northeastern Morainal Natural Division** is the most recently glaciated in Illinois. Drainage is poor, thus marshes, natural lakes, and bogs are distinctive features. With diverse wetland, prairie, forest, savanna, and lake communities, this northeastern section of Illinois hosts the greatest biodiversity in Illinois, as well as the largest human population.

4. The **Grand Prairie Natural Division** of central and east-central Illinois is the largest natural division in the state, and is a vast plain formerly occupied primarily by tallgrass prairie, now converted extensively to agriculture. Natural drainage of the fertile soils was poor, resulting in many marshes and potholes.

5. The **Western Forest-Prairie Natural Division** of west-central Illinois is a dissected glacial till plain. Forests were the predominant vegetation, with prairie on the level uplands. Today, forests remain in the riparian areas and on steep hillsides, while the former prairie has been converted for agriculture.

6. The **Illinois River and Mississippi River Sand Areas Natural Division** is home to sandy areas and dunes in the Illinois and Mississippi River bottomlands. On drier sites, sand prairie and scrub oak woods were typical.

7. The **Upper Mississippi River and Illinois River Bottomlands Natural Division** of western and west-central Illinois features large river floodplains and gravel terraces. Most of the Division was originally forest, with smaller areas of prairie, marsh, and moist savanna.

8. The **Middle Mississippi Border Natural Division** of west-central Illinois features river bluffs and rugged terrain bordering the Mississippi River floodplain from Rock Island County to St. Clair County and the lower Illinois floodplain. Major vegetation types include oak-hickory forests, limestone glades, and loess and glacial till prairie.

9. The **Ozark Natural Division** consists of the part of the Ozark uplift that extends into southwestern Illinois. Topography is a dissected plateau with bluffs along the Mississippi River, and a sinkhole plain in the northern section. Natural vegetation of the area is mostly forested with many hill prairies.

10. The **Southern Till Plain Natural Division** of south-central Illinois, the state's second largest division, is a dissected plain south of the terminal Wisconsinan moraine. Forest was found along streams, and prairie occupied the level uplands. Soils are poor because of high clay content and frequent "claypan" subsoils. Post oak flatwoods are characteristic.

11. The **Wabash Border Natural Division** includes the bottomlands and the loess-covered uplands bordering the Wabash River and its major tributaries in southeastern Illinois. Lowland oak forests with beech, tuliptree and other eastern species are characteristic, with smaller areas of wet prairies, sloughs, and marshes.

12. The **Lower Mississippi River Bottomlands Natural Division** includes

the Mississippi River and its floodplain from Alton to the Thebes Gorge. Natural vegetation included prairies, marshes, and rich forests with several southern lowland tree species.

13. The **Shawnee Hills Natural Division** extends across the southern tip of Illinois. The unglaciated hill country is characterized by an east-west escarpment of sandstone cliffs and a series of lower hills. Originally, the division was mostly forested, and is presently the most heavily forested of Illinois' natural divisions.

14. The **Coastal Plain Natural Division** of extreme southern Illinois is a region of swampy forested bottomlands and low clay and gravel hills. Bald cypress-tupelo swamps are a unique feature. The floodplain at the confluence of the Mississippi and Ohio rivers and Cache and Ohio rivers support rich bottomland forests.

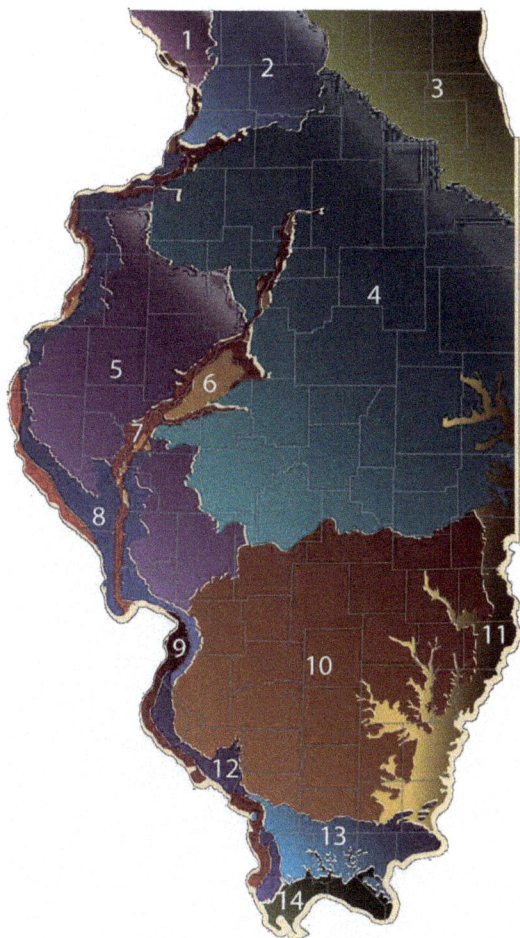

Illinois Natural Divisions

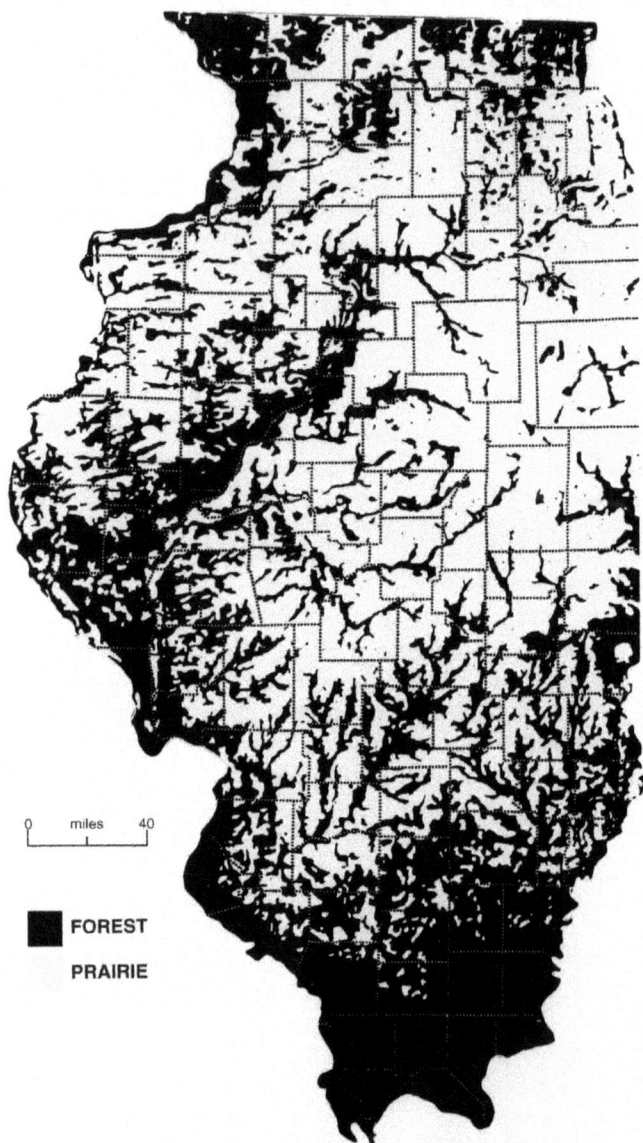

Approximate extent of forest and prairie vegetation in presettlement Illinois.

WHORLED MILKWEED
Asclepias quadrifolia Jacq.

Asclepias Named for *Asklepios,* the god of healing in Greek mythology.

Stems Upright, unbranched, smooth or a little hairy, up to 2 feet tall.

Leaves Whorled, or some of them opposite; simple; lanceolate to ovate, without teeth, up to 6 inches long, less than ½ as wide, on short stalks.

Flower arrangement Several in 1–4 terminal umbels.

Flowers Up to ¼-inch across, on slender stalks up to 1 inch long.

Sepals 5, united at the base, green.

Petals 5, pink, turned downward.

Stamens and pistil Associated together with a central column of 5 pink hoods, each hood with a curved horn protruding from it.

KEY FACTS

Perennial from slender rhizomes; stems and leaves with milky sap.

Habitat Rocky open woods, upland slopes and ridges

Flowering early May to early July

Fruit Follicles upright, up to 5 inches long, smooth.

Note This is the first milkweed to bloom in Illinois. Like most milkweeds, this one has milky sap.

SLEEPY CATCHFLY
Silene antirrhina L.

KEY FACTS

Annual from very slender roots.

Habitat Woods, prairies, fields, roadsides, along railroads

Flowering late April until the end of summer

Silene From From *Silenus,* a mythological character covered with foam, in allusion to the viscid excretions of many of these plants.

Flower arrangement Several in a terminal cluster.

Flowers Up to 1/6-inch across, on short stalks. **Sepals** United into a swollen, ovoid, 5-toothed cup up to ¼-inch long. **Petals** 5, pale pink, notched at the tip, about 1/6-inch long, withering rapidly, or often absent entirely. **Stamens** 10. **Pistil** Ovary superior, styles 3.

Fruit Capsule opening by means of teeth at the tip; seeds numerous.

Note The sticky areas on the stems traps ants, gnats, and other small insects, but the plant does not receive any nourishment from them.

Stems Upright, slender, smooth or minutely hairy, with a sticky area just below the attachment of each pair of leaves.

Leaves Opposite, the lowest ones spatulate, stalked, up to 2 inches long, the upper ones linear, without stalks, smaller than the basal leaves.

FIREPINK
Silene virginica L.

Stems Upright, branched, sticky-hairy, up to 2 feet tall.

Leaves Opposite, simple, without teeth, hairy, the lower ones spatulate rounded at the tip, tapering to a stalk, up to 4 inches long, the upper ones lanceolate, pointed at the tip, tapering to the sessile base, to 2½ inches long.

Flower arrangement Several in a branched, terminal cluster.

Flowers Up to 1½ inches broad, on sticky-hairy stalks. **Sepals** Cup-shaped below, 5-parted near the tip, green, sticky-hairy, up to ¾-inch long. **Petals** 5, free from each other, notched at the tip, crimson, up to 1½ inches long. **Stamens** 10. **Pistil** Ovary superior, styles 3.

Fruit Capsule opening by a few teeth at the top, with several warty seeds.

KEY FACTS

Perennial from woody base and branched rootstock.

Habitat Bottomland and mesic forests, streambanks, base of bluffs, pastures

Flowering mid-April to late May

Use This attractive plant is well-suited to the wildflower garden.

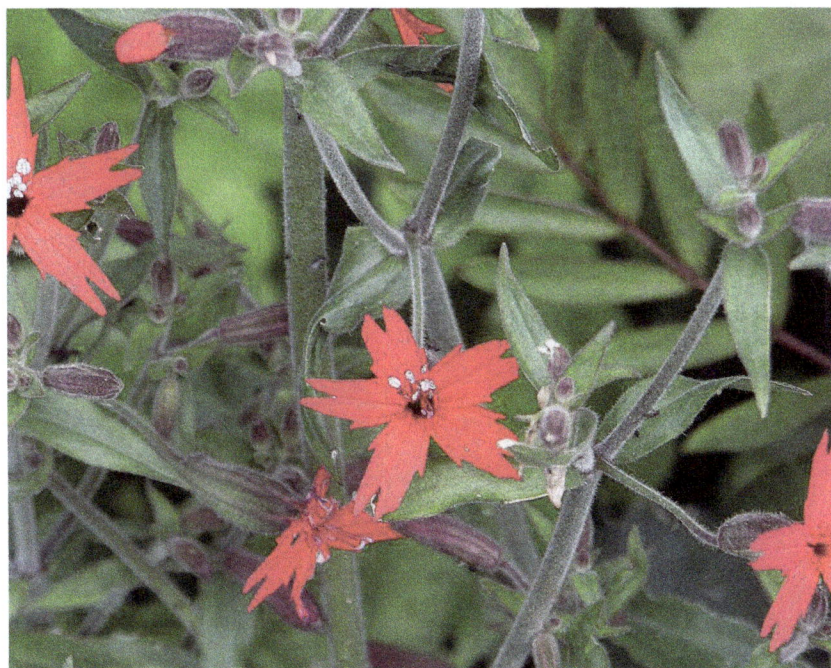

BUFFALO CLOVER

Trifolium reflexum L.

PEA FAMILY | FABACEAE

Annual or biennial from a small taproot.

Habitat Uncommon in rocky woods, prairies, savannas, streambanks; soils typically acidic.

Flowering mid-May to August

Stems Spreading or ascending, branched, usually hairy, up to 15 inches long.

Leaves Divided into 3 leaflets, the leaflets oval, rounded at the tip, tapering to the base, sharply but finely toothed, up to 1 inch long.

Flower arrangement Many in dense, round heads up to 1¼ inch in diameter.

Trifolium Latin, *tres*, three, and *folium*, leaf.

Flowers Up to ½-inch long, pea-shaped, on reflexed stalks. **Sepals** 5, green, united below, minutely hairy. **Petals** 5, the back one red, the others white. **Stamens** 10, united below. **Pistil** Ovary superior.

Fruit Pod elongated, up to ¼-inch long, usually with 3–6 seeds.

Note The petals turn brown shortly after flowering. May be confused with **red clover** (*Trifolium pratense*); the flower head of buffalo clover sits well above the leaves, where the head of red clover appears to be resting on the leaves. Also, during and shortly after flowering, the lower portion of the flowers of buffalo clover hang downward or droop.

RED COLUMBINE
Aquilegia canadensis L.

Aquilegia *Aquila*, eagle, from the resemblance of the spurs to claws.

Stems Upright, smooth or somewhat hairy, branched, up to 2 feet tall.

Leaves Basal leaves doubly compound, long-stalked, the leaflets smooth or slightly hairy, round-toothed, pale on the lower surface; stem-leaves divided, without stalks.

Flower arrangement Several in terminal racemes.

Flowers Up to 2½ inches long, nodding, on slender stalks. **Sepals** 5, petal-like, falling away early. **Petals** 5, projected backwards into 5 hollow spurs, red on the outside, yellow inside, the spurs up to ½-inch long and swollen at the tip. **Stamens** Many, protruding from the flower. **Pistils** 5, the ovary superior, the style protruding from the flower.

Fruit Clusters of 5 follicles, up to 2/3-inch long, with slender beaks.

Note This species makes a handsome addition to a wildflower garden. This is the only columbine native to Illinois.

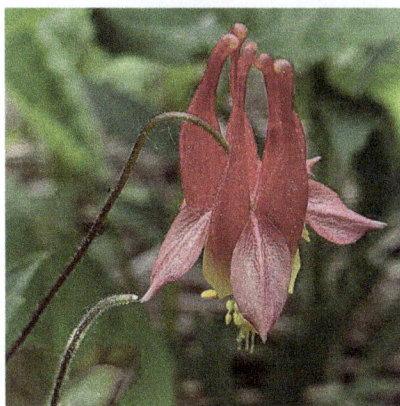

KEY FACTS

Perennial from thickened roots.

Habitat Rocky, open woods and slopes; limestone glades, low woods

Flowering mid-April to late May

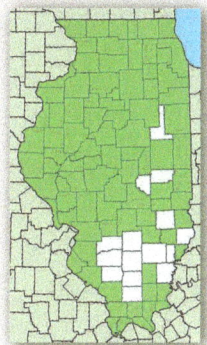

PINK VALERIAN
Valeriana pauciflora Michx.

KEY FACTS

Perennial from rather slender roots.

Habitat Floodplain woods, shaded ravines

Flowering late April to mid-May

Valeriana The medieval name.

Flower arrangement Many in a terminal cluster.

Flowers Up to 1 inch long, on slender, smooth stalks. **Sepals** United into a small tube, green. **Petals** 5, united into a long tube, pink. **Stamens** Usually 4, attached to the tube of the petals. **Pistil** Ovary inferior.

Fruit Dry, oblong, up to ¼-inch long.

Stems Upright, smooth, up to 2½ feet tall, often with runners at the base.

Leaves Basal and opposite, smooth, the basal ones simple, ovate, heart-shaped at the base, round-toothed, the stem-leaves pinnately divided into 3–7 segments, the terminal segment usually much larger than the others.

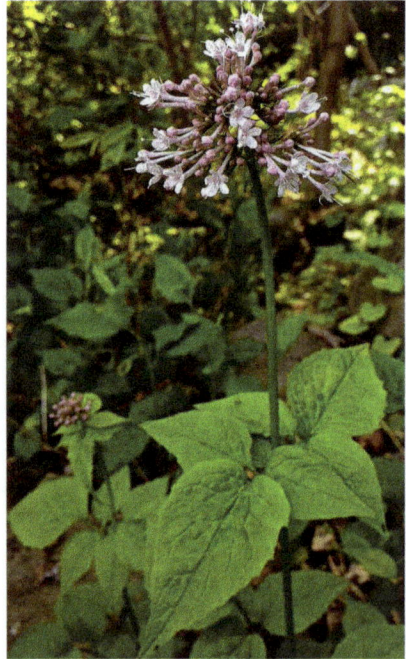

BLACK SNAKEROOT

Sanicula odorata (Raf.) K.M. Pryer & L.R. Phillippe

Sanicula Latin, *sanare*, to heal.

Synonym *Sanicula gregaria* Bicknell

Stems Upright, branched, smooth, up to 2 feet tall.

Leaves Alternate or basal, palmately compound with 5 leaflets, the leaflets lanceolate, pointed at the tip, tapering to the base, sharply toothed, smooth.

Flower arrangement Several flowers in umbels.

Flowers Up to 1/6-inch long, short-stalked, perfect or bearing only stamens. **Sepals** 5, small, united below. **Petals** 5, yellow, longer than the sepals. **Stamens** 5, with bright yellow anthers. **Pistil** Ovary inferior, styles 2.

Fruit Up to 1/6-inch long, covered with hooked bristles, the persistent

KEY FACTS
Perennial from fibrous roots.

Habitat Rich woods, thickets, seeps

Flowering mid-April to early June

styles shorter than the bristles of the fruit.

Note There are three additional species of *Sanicula* in Illinois very similar to black snakeroot.

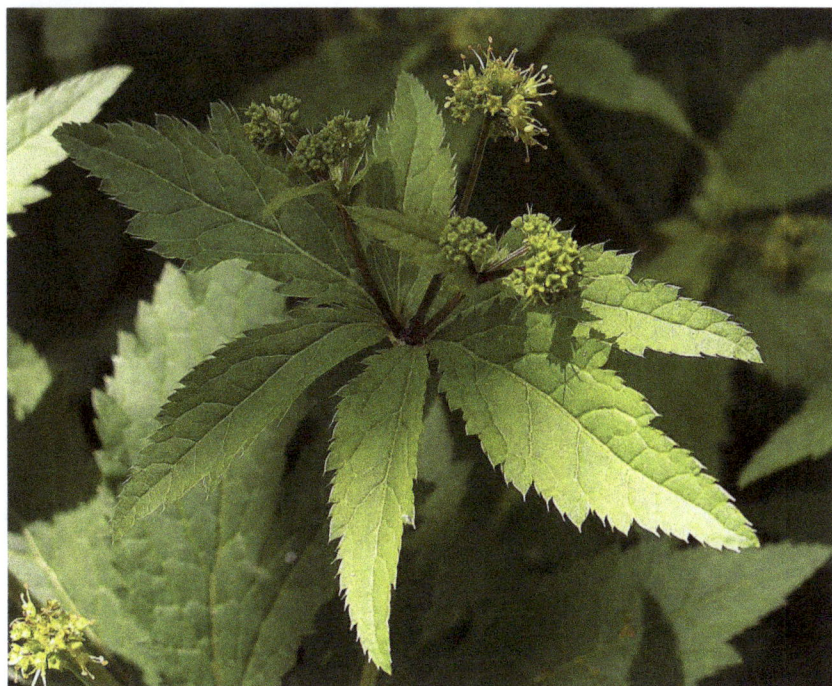

YELLOW PIMPERNEL
Taenidia integerrima (L.) Drude

KEY FACTS

Perennial from tufted roots.

Habitat Dry rocky woods; dry prairies, bluffs and savannas

Flowering May and June

Stems Upright, smooth, branched, to 3 feet tall.

Leaves Pinnately divided, with each of the 3 divisions divided again into 3–5 leaflets, on long stalks swollen at the base, the leaflets ovate to oval, without teeth, up to 1 inch long, smooth.

Taenidia Greek, *tainidion*, a narrow strip, from the small rib.

Flower arrangement Several in umbels on 10–20 very slender, smooth stalks.

Flowers Up to ¼-inch across, each on a slender individual stalk. **Sepals** United into a minute cup, with the lobes virtually non-existent. **Petals** 5, yellow, free from each other. **Stamens** 5, very short. **Pistils** Ovary inferior, styles 2.

Fruit Oval, up to 1/6-inch long, smooth.

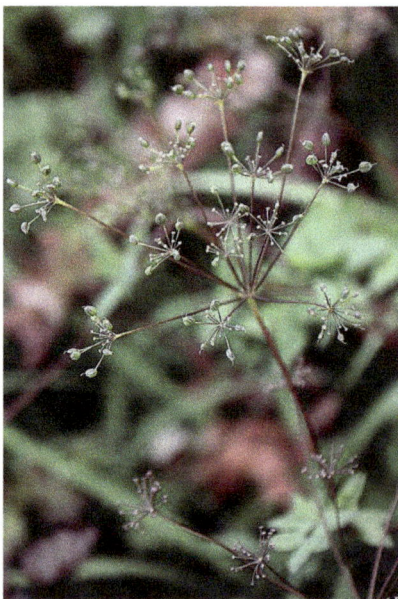

MEADOW PARSNIP
Thaspium trifoliatum (L.) Gray

Thaspium Anagram of *Thapsia*, a related genus.

Stems Upright, branched, smooth, to 1½ feet tall.

Leaves Basal leaves simple and broadly ovate or divided into 3 leaflets, long-stalked; stem-leaves 3-divided, the leaflets ovate to narrowly ovate, toothed, smooth, up to 2 inches long.

Flower arrangement Many, in several-rayed umbels.

Flowers Up to 1/6-inch across, on slender, smooth stalks. **Sepals** 5, green, united below. **Petals** 5, yellow or purple, free from each other. **Stamens** 5. **Pistil** Ovary inferior; styles 2, slender.

KEY FACTS

Perennial from tufted roots.

Habitat Rocky woods, bluffs, prairies, oak savannas

Flowering late April to early June

Fruit More or less flattened, winged, about 1/6-inch long, smooth.

Note The yellow-flowered form and the purple-flowered form frequently occur together.

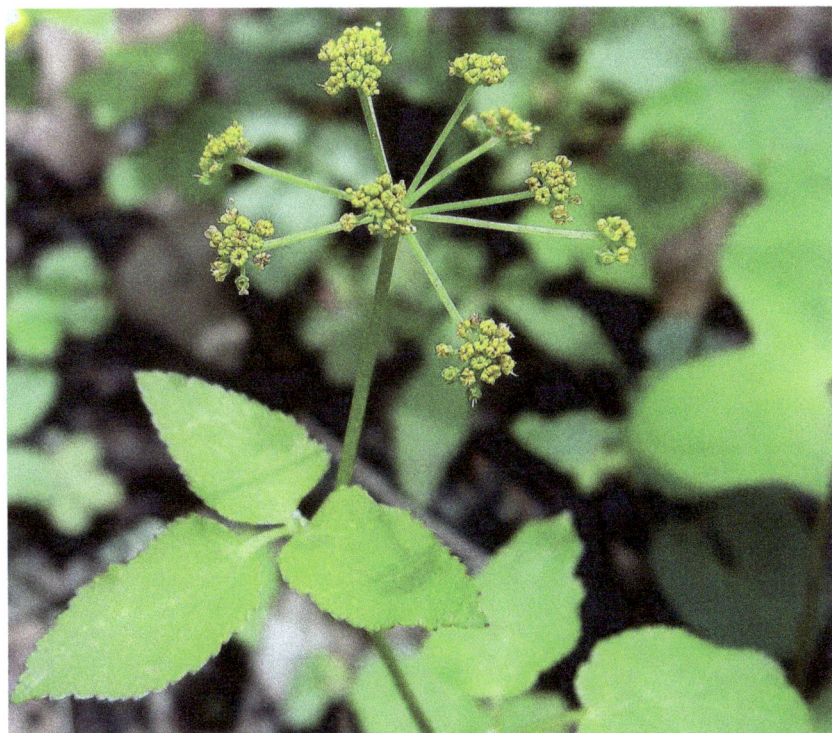

FALSE DANDELION

Krigia biflora (Walt.) Blake

ASTER FAMILY | ASTERACEAE

Perennial from a thickened root.

Habitat Sandy woods, oak savannas, prairies

Flowering May until early September

Krigia Named for David Krig, a German physician, and an early plant collector in Maryland.

Flower arrangement Many crowded into 2 or more heads, the heads up to 1½ inches across, on long stalks, each head subtended by a series of green bracts.

Flowers All ray-like. **Sepals** None. **Petals** United into slender yellow-orange rays. **Stamens** 5. **Pistil** Ovary inferior, surrounded by several white hairs.

Fruit Achenes, with a tuft of white hairs at the tip.

Note This false dandelion differs from *Krigia dandelion* by having more than 1 head of flowers.

Stems Upright, smooth, usually bluish, up to 2 feet tall, bearing 1 leaf.

Leaves All basal except one on the stem, elliptic, up to 7 inches long, shallowly toothed or almost wavy-edged, smooth, the basal leaves on stalks.

WILD FALSE DANDELION

Krigia dandelion (L.) Nutt.

Stems Leaf-bearing stems absent.

Leaves Basal, narrowly lanceolate, up to 6 inches long, without teeth or with an occasional coarse tooth or even shallowly lobed, smooth.

Flower arrangement Many flowers in a solitary head on a leafless stalk up to 1½ feet tall.

Flowers Each flower ray-like, crowded in a flattened head, subtended by numerous scales, the head up to 1 inch broad. **Sepals** None. **Petals** United into a strap-shaped ray with 5 small teeth at the tip, yellow. **Stamens** 5. **Pistil** Ovary

KEY FACTS

Perennial from slender roots and occasional tubers; stems with milky sap.

Habitat Woods, prairies, fields, roadsides

Flowering late April to late May

inferior, subtended by numerous silky hairs.

Fruit Achenes with silky hairs attached.

Note This species contains milky sap.

GOLDEN RAGWORT
Packera aurea (L.) A. & D. Löve

KEY FACTS

Perennial from tufted roots.

Habitat Low woods, shorelines, old fields; tolerant of shade

Flowering mid-April to early June

Synonym *Senecio aureus* L.

Stems Upright, smooth, to 2 feet tall.

Leaves Basal and alternate, smooth, the basal ovate with a heart-shaped base, round-toothed, up to 6 inches long, on long stalks; stem-leaves lanceolate, some of them pinnately lobed, the uppermost usually without a stalk.

Packera Named for John Packer, 20th century botanist.

Flower arrangement Many in a head, with several heads in a terminal cluster, each head subtended by small, leaf-like bracts.

Flowers Two kinds, one of them ray-like, the other tubular and forming a central disk, both of them golden yellow. **Sepals** None. **Petals** Ray-like or tubular, golden yellow. **Stamens** 5. **Pistil** Ovary inferior, surrounded by white hairs.

Fruit Achenes smooth, with a tuft of white hairs at the top.

Notes This plant is reportedly poisonous to cattle. The simple, heart-shaped basal leaves contrast with the pinnately divided stem-leaves.

BUTTERWEED
Packera glabella (Poir.) C. Jeffrey

Synonym *Senecio glabellus* Poir.

Stems Upright, usually smooth, sometimes branched, hollow, up to 3 feet tall.

Leaves Alternate, deeply pinnately divided into 3–13 segments, each segment usually toothed, smooth, the lower leaves on long stalks, the upper leaves on short stalks or no stalks at all.

Flower arrangement Many flowers in a head, with several heads in terminal clusters, each head subtended by small green bracts.

Flowers Two kinds, one ray-like, the other tubular and forming a central disk, both of them yellow. **Sepals** None. **Petals** Some united into rays, other united into short tubes. **Stamens** 4. **Pistil** Ovary inferior, surrounded by white hairs.

Fruit Achenes smooth, with a tuft of white hairs at the top.

KEY FACTS

Annual from slender roots.

Habitat Low woods, swamps, and other wetlands.

Flowering mid-April to early June

Note Sometimes forming large colonies in disturbed areas, especially in agricultural fields during a wet spring.

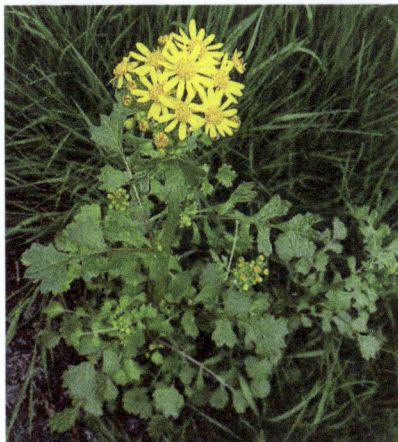

HOARY PUCCOON

BORAGE FAMILY | BORAGINACEAE

Lithospermum canescens (Michx.) Lehm.

Perennial from a thickened root which contains red sap.

Habitat Dry woods, savannas, prairies

Flowering late March to early June

Lithospermum Greek, *lithos*, stone, and *sperma*, seed, in allusion to the hard nutlets.

Flowers Up to ½-inch across, on short, hairy stalks. **Sepals** 5, narrow, united below into a tube, hairy. **Petals** 5, united below, orange, very showy. **Stamens** 5, attached to the tube of the petals. **Pistil** Ovary 4-parted, superior.

Fruit A cluster of 4 white shiny, smooth nutlets.

Use The red sap in roots may be used as a dye.

Stems Upright, often branched, hairy, up to 1½ feet tall.

Leaves Alternate, simple, narrowly oblong, without teeth, hairy, up to 1½ inches long, less than ½-inch wide.

Flower arrangement Several in dense, terminal racemes.

AMERICAN GROMWELL
Lithospermum latifolium Michx.

Other name PEARL SEED.

Stems Upright, branched, hairy, to 3 feet tall.

Leaves Alternate, simple, ovate to ovate-lanceolate, without teeth, hairy, to 5 inches long, to 2 inches broad.

Flower arrangement 1-few from the axils of the leaves.

Flowers Up to ¼-inch across, on very short, hairy stalks. **Sepals** 5, narrow, united at the base, green, hairy. **Petals** 5, united below into a short funnel, pale yellow, just barely longer than the sepals. **Stamens** 5, attached to the petals. **Pistil** Ovary superior, 4-parted.

Fruit Nutlet pearly white, shiny, ovoid, up to 1/6-inch long.

Note The pearly white nutlets are a unique feature of this genus.

KEY FACTS

Perennial from slender roots.

Habitat Rich woods, shaded riverbanks

Flowering May to early June

YELLOW BELLWORT
AUTUMN-CROCUS FAMILY | COLCHICACEAE
Uvularia grandiflora Sm.

Perennial from thickened roots.

Habitat Rich woods, riverbanks, shaded seeps

Flowering mid-April to mid-May

Stems Upright, smooth, often branched, up to 1½ feet tall.

Leaves Alternate, simple, oblong to oval, without teeth, smooth, up to 4 inches long, seemingly pierced near the base by the stem.

Uvularia From "flowers hanging like the *uvula*, or palate."

Flower arrangement Solitary from the tip of the stem.

Flowers Up to 1½ inches long, drooping, on a curved, smooth stalk. **Perianth** 6-parted, the sepals and petals not distinguishable, yellow, lanceolate. **Stamens** 6. **Pistils** Ovary superior, 3-lobed; styles 3, united below.

Fruit Capsules 3-angled, up to ½-inch long, smooth, with few seeds.

Use The starchy roots may be cooked and eaten.

Note This is an attractive species for the wildflower garden.

Hypoxis hirsuta (L.) Coville

Hypoxis Greek, *hypoxys*, somewhat acid.

Stems Leaf-bearing stems absent.
Leaves All basal, long and narrow, up to ¼-inch wide, conspicuously hairy.
Flower arrangement 1–6 in an umbel, borne at the tip of a leafless stem.
Flowers Up to ¾-inch across, on slender, hairy stalks. **Perianth** 6-parted, the sepals and petals not distinguishable, bright yellow, oblong to lanceolate. **Stamens** 6, attached to the very base of the perianth parts. **Pistils** Ovary inferior, 3-lobed; stigmas 3.

KEY FACTS

Perennial from an underground corm.

Habitat Dry, rocky woods; savannas, prairies

Flowering late April to late May

Fruit Capsule nearly round, up to 1/6-inch in diameter, with several black seeds.
Use This species is ideal in a rock garden.

YELLOW DOG'S-TOOTH VIOLET

LILY FAMILY | LILIACEAE

Erythronium americanum Ker-Gawl.

Perennial from a deep corm.

Habitat Rich woods, streambanks

Flowering late March to May

Erythronium Greek, *erythros*, red, the European species being red-flowered.

Flowers Nodding, up to 2 inches long. **Perianth parts** 6, oblong, yellow, up to 2 inches long, speckled inside. **Stamens** 6, shorter than the perianth parts. **Pistil** Ovary superior, style 3-parted.

Fruit Capsule obovoid, tapering to a narrowed base, smooth, up to 1 inch long, with several curved seeds.

Other Names YELLOW TROUT LILY, YELLOW ADDER'S-TONGUE.

Stems No leaf-bearing stem present.

Leaves 1 or 2, basal, oblong-lanceolate, pointed at the tip, tapering to the base, smooth, mottled, up to 8 inches long, up to 2 inches broad.

Flower arrangement Solitary on a stalk up to 10 inches long.

Use The leaves of this plant can be par-boiled, seasoned, and eaten as a vegetable.

Note It is nearly impossible to tell this species from white dog's-tooth violet (*Erythronium albidum* Nutt.) unless the flower is present.

YELLOW LADIES'-SLIPPER

Cypripedium parviflorum var. *pubescens* (Willd.) Knight

Cypripedium *Cypris*, Venus, and *pedilon*, shoe.

Synonyms *Cypripedium calceolus* L. var. *pubescens* (Willd.) Correll, *Cypripedium pubescens* Willd.

Stems Upright, unbranched, hairy, up to 2 feet tall.

Leaves Alternate, broadly elliptic, pointed at the tip, hairy, up to 6 inches long and up to 3 inches broad.

Flower arrangement 1–few at the tip of the stem.

Flowers Up to 2½ inches long, drooping. **Sepals** 3, yellow or green and striped with purple, broadly lanceolate, up to 2½ inches long. **Petals** 3, the lateral 2 narrow and twisted, the lip slipper-shaped, yellow with purple stripes, up to 2 inches long. **Stamen** 1, triangular. **Pistil** Ovary inferior, stigma triangular.

Fruit Capsule elliptic, with minute seeds.

Note This beautiful species is becoming quite rare in the state.

KEY FACTS

Perennial from a tuft of thick roots.

Habitat Moist to dry woods, forested bogs

Flowering Last week in April until late May

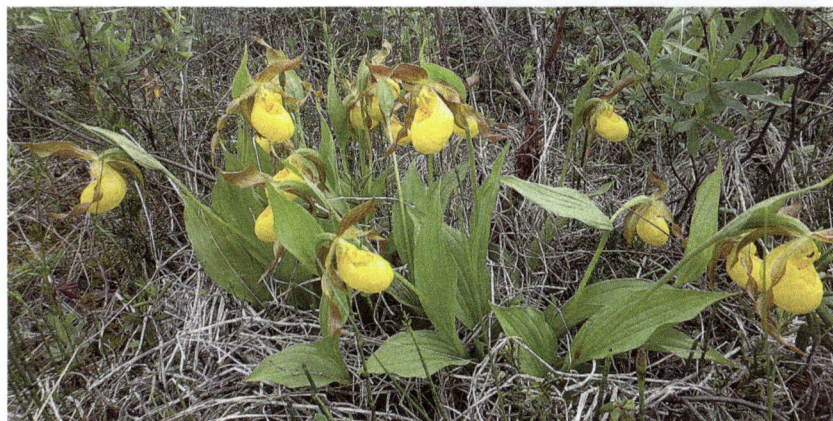

LOUSEWORT
Pedicularis canadensis L.

BROOM-RAPE FAMILY | OROBANCHACEAE

KEY FACTS

Perennial from a thickened root.

Habitat Open dry woods, oak savannas, prairies

Flowering late April to late May

Other name WOOD BETONY

Stems Upright, hairy, up to 15 inches tall.

Leaves Basal and alternate or even sometimes opposite, pinnately lobed into 5–19 lobes, hairy, up to 6 inches long, all but the uppermost stalked.

Flower arrangement Several in terminal spikes.

Pedicularis Latin, *pediculus*, a louse, from the early European belief that livestock became infested with lice from grazing in fields containing this plant.

Flowers Up to 1 inch long, without stalks. **Sepals** United into an asymmetrical, short cup, green. **Petals** 5, united below into tube, yellow, the lobes divided into 2 lips, the upper lip forming a hood, the lower lip 3-lobed. **Stamens** 4, attached to the petals. **Pistil** Ovary superior.

Fruit Capsule lanceolate, up to ⅔-inch long.

Use This is a handsome species for the wildflower garden.

Note *Pedicularis* is partially parasitic on the roots of other plants, but still produced chlorophyll on its own.

YELLOW WOOD SORREL
Oxalis stricta L.

Oxalis Greek, *oxys, sour.*

Other name SHEEP SORREL.

Stems Upright, branched, smooth or with appressed hairs, up to 10 inches tall.

Leaves Divided into 3 leaflets, the leaflets broadest at the notched tip, up to 1½ inches broad, smooth or somewhat hairy.

Flower arrangement Several in terminal clusters resembling umbels.

Flowers Up to ½-inch long, on slender stalks. **Sepals** 5, green, narrow, less than half as long as the petals. **Petals** 5, yellow, often with a reddish center, free from each other. **Stamens** 10. **Pistil** Ovary superior, 5-lobed; styles 5.

Fruit Capsule elongated, smooth, tapering to a beak, to 1¼ inches long.

KEY FACTS

Perennial from slender rootstocks.

Habitat Woods, fields, roadsides

Flowering late April until mid-autumn

Use Used sparingly, the sour leaves may be added to salads.

Note Some purple-leaved forms are found in Illinois.

YELLOW CORYDALIS
Corydalis flavula (Raf.) DC.

KEY FACTS

Annual from slender roots.

Habitat Low, moist woods

Flowering early April to late May

Corydalis The ancient Greek name for the crested lark.

smooth, the lowermost on long stalks, the uppermost with short or no stalks.

Flower arrangement Several flowers in racemes.

Flowers One-fourth to one-third inch long. **Sepals** 2, green, small, falling off early. **Petals** 4, yellow, one of them protruding at the base into a spur, the inner petals with a toothed ridge down their back. **Stamens** 6, in two sets of 3. **Pistil** Ovary superior.

Fruit Elongated capsule, constricted between the seeds, smooth, up to 1½ inches long.

Stems Spreading to more or less upright, much branched, smooth, slender, to 10 inches long.

Leaves Alternate, much divided and almost "fern-like," gray green,

CELANDINE POPPY

Stylophorum diphyllum (Michx.) Nutt.

Stylophorum Greek, *stylos*, style and *phoros*, bearing.

Stems More or less upright, hairy, with yellow sap, to about 12 inches tall.

Leaves Both at the base of the plant and along the stem, pinnately lobed, with each lobe toothed, hairy, up to 10 inches long.

Flower arrangement 1–4 in clusters at the tip of the stem.

Flowers Up to 2 inches across, on hairy stalks. **Sepals** 2, green, hairy, falling away very early. **Petals** 4, bright yellow, ½–1 inch long, rounded at the tip. **Stamens** Several to many. **Pistil** Ovary superior, stigma 2- to 3-parted.

Fruit Ovoid, white-hairy capsule, up to 1 inch long.

Use This species is an attractive plant for shaded wildflower gardens.

KEY FACTS

Perennial from a stout rootstock.

Habitat Rich, moist woods; ravines, rocky streambanks

Flowering mid-April through much of May

BRISTLY BUTTERCUP

Ranunculus hispidus Michx.

BUTTERCUP FAMILY | RANUNCULACEAE

KEY FACTS

Perennial from tufted roots.

Habitat Dry woods, oak bluffs

Flowering late March to late May

Ranunculus Latin for "little frog," applied by Pliny to these plants, some of which grow in wet places.

Flowers Up to 1¼ inch broad, on densely hairy stalks. **Sepals** 5, green. **Petals** 5, yellow, about twice as long as the sepals. **Stamens** Numerous, surrounding the pistils. **Pistils** Numerous, clustered in the center of the flower.

Fruit Achenes clustered in a head, each achene beaked.

Stem Upright, branched, densely hairy, to 20 inches tall.

Leaves Basal and alternate, pinnately compound with 3–5 leaflets, the leaflets lobed or sharply toothed, narrowed to the base, densely hairy.

Flower arrangement Few in terminal racemes.

Note **Bristly buttercup** and **swamp buttercup** (*R. septentrionalis*) are very similar to each other. Bristly buttercup has long, spreading hairs on its stems and leaf stalks, and is found in drier habitats than swamp buttercup. Swamp buttercup is either hairless or has only short, appressed hairs along its stems and leaf stalks. Some references treat these two buttercups as one species.

WOODLAND CROWFOOT

Ranunculus micranthus Nutt.

Stems Upright, branched, usually hairy, at least at the base, up to 15 inches tall.

Leaves Usually hairy, the basal leaves ovate to orbicular, unlobed or 3-lobed, round-toothed, on long stalks, the stem-leaves each with 3 narrow, sometimes toothed, divisions.

Flower arrangement Few in branched, terminal clusters.

Flowers About ¼-inch broad, on long stalks. **Sepals** 5, green, narrow. **Petals** 5, yellow, rounded at the tip, about as long as the sepals. **Stamens** Several, surrounding the cluster of pistils. **Pistils** Several, arranged in a central "cone," the ovaries superior.

KEY FACTS

Perennial from rather fleshy roots.

Habitat Moist woods, marshes, swamps

Flowering mid-March to mid-May

Fruit A cone-shaped cluster of achenes, each achene rather plump.

Note This species closely resembles the **small-flowered crowfoot** (*Ranunculus abortivus*), but usually can be distinguished by its hairy stems.

ROUGH CROWFOOT
Ranunculus recurvatus Poir.

Perennial from fibrous roots.

Habitat Floodplain woods, seeps and depressions, swamps

Flowering May to early June

Flowers Up to ½-inch broad, on hairy stalks. **Sepals** 5, green, turned downward. **Petals** 5, pale yellow, about as long as or shorter than the sepals. **Stamens** Numerous, surrounding the pistils. **Pistils** Many in a cluster in the center of the flower.

Fruit Achenes in a cluster up to ½-inch wide, each achene with a short, curved beak.

Other names BLISTERWORT, HOOKED BUTTERCUP.

Stems Upright, branched, hairy, to 18 inches tall.

Leaves Basal and alternate, hairy, deeply 3-lobed, up to 3 inches across, each lobe toothed or even lobed again.

Flower arrangement Few in a terminal cluster.

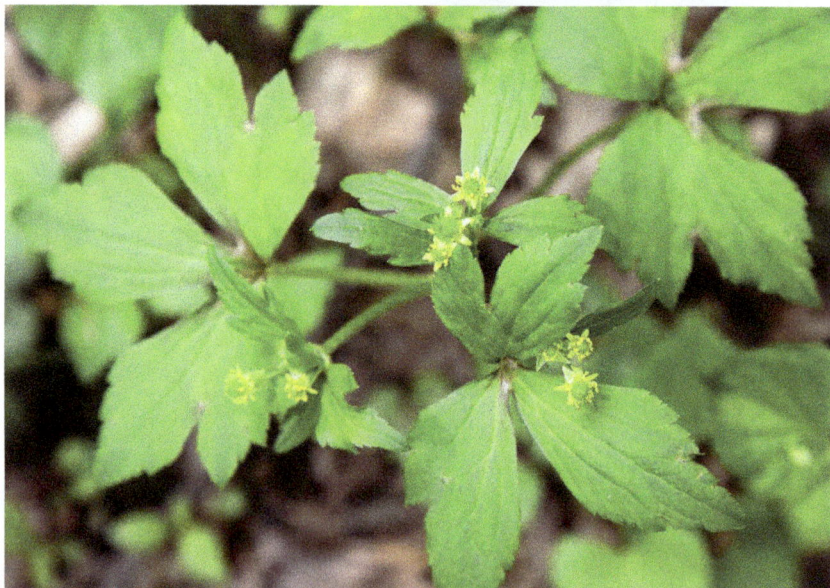

SWAMP BUTTERCUP

Ranunculus septentrionalis Poir.

Stems Upright to sprawling, branched, usually smooth, to 2 feet long.

Leaves All 3-parted, with each part further divided and toothed, usually smooth, the lower leaves on longer stalks than the upper.

Flower arrangement 1–several in branched, terminal clusters.

Flowers Up to 1½ inches broad, on usually smooth stalks. **Sepals** 5, green, smooth, about half as long as the petals. **Petals** Usually 5, bright yellow, waxy, broadly rounded at the tip. **Stamens** Several, surrounding the pistils. **Pistils** Several, in a central cone, the ovaries superior.

Fruit Many achenes grouped in a central "cone," each achene flat, with a narrow wing and a short, slender beak.

KEY FACTS

Perennial from fibrous roots

Habitat Moist woods, marshes, swamps, seeps

Flowering mid-April to early June, often again in fall

Note Similar to **bristly buttercup**, (*R. hispidus*) and sometimes considered a variety of that species. However, the stems of bristly buttercup have abundant spreading hairs and they are usually more erect than the more or less smooth, often sprawling stems of swamp buttercup.

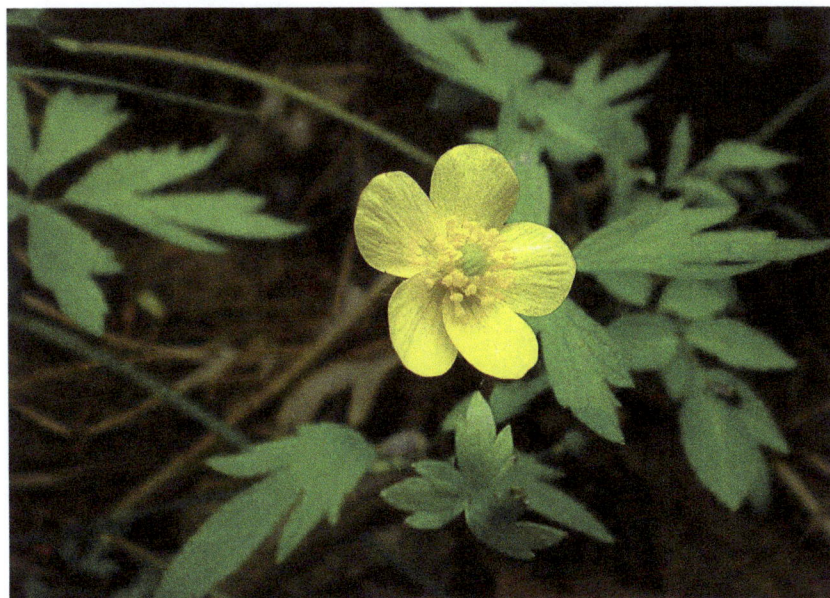

SPRING AVENS

Geum vernum (Raf.) Torr. & Gray

KEY FACTS

Perennial from fibrous roots.

Habitat Mesic to moist woods, wet ground, seeps.

Flowering Most of April and May

Stems Upright, usually unbranched, mostly hairy, up to 21 inches tall.

Leaves Basal leaves simple and 3 to 5-lobed or pinnately compound with 3–9 leaflets, coarsely toothed, hairy, on long stalks; stem-leaves al-

Geum Ancient name for some plant.

ternate, lobed or pinnately compound, with no stalk.

Flower arrangement 1-several in a terminal cluster.

Flowers ¼-inch broad, stalked. **Sepals** 5, united below, the lobes turned downward. **Petals** 5, yellow, longer than the sepals. **Stamens** Many, surrounding the pistils. **Pistils** Many in a central cluster; style long and very slender.

Fruit A beard of long-beaked achenes raised on a stalk above the persistent sepals.

Note The stalked head of fruits is distinctive.

COMMON CINQUEFOIL
Potentilla simplex Michx.

Potentilla Diminutive of *potens*, powerful, in reference to supposed medicinal powers.

Other name FIVE-FINGER.

Stems Spreading or lying on the ground, hairy, up to 2 feet long.

Leaves All but the uppermost palmately compound with 5 leaflets, the leaflets oblong, coarsely toothed, hairy on the lower surface, up to 2½ inches long.

Flower arrangement Solitary from the axils of the leaves.

Flowers Up to ½-inch broad, on long, hairy stalks. **Sepals** 5, green, united at the base. **Petals** 5, yellow, broadest at the rounded tip.

KEY FACTS

Perennial from a short rootstock.

Habitat Rocky woods, savannas, fields, prairies

Flowering late April to mid-June

Stamens 20 or more. **Pistils** Several, clustered in the center of the flower.

Fruit Clustered, with an elongated beak.

SMOOTH YELLOW VIOLET

Viola pubescens Ait.

Perennial from a cluster of roots.

Habitat Mesic woods, thickets, woodland borders

Flowering late March to mid-May

Stems Upright, smooth or barely hairy near the top, up to 10 inches tall, usually several from the base of each plant.

Leaves Basal or alternate, broadly ovate, heart-shaped at the base,

Viola The ancient name.

with low, rounded teeth, smooth except for some hairs on the veins and margins, up to 2 inches across, the basal leaves on longer stalks.

Flower arrangement Solitary from the axils of the upper leaves.

Flowers Up to 1½ inches long, on smooth stalks. **Sepals** 5, green, smooth, narrow. **Petals** 5, yellow, sometimes with a few purple stripes, the lateral petals with a beard of hairs within. **Stamens** 5. **Pistil** Ovary superior.

Fruit Capsule smooth or woolly, with several brown seeds.

Use This is an attractive plant for wildflower gardens.

WILD PETUNIA
Ruellia pedunculata Torr. ex Gray

Ruellia For Jean Ruelle, 1474-1537, French herbalist.

Stems Upright, hairy, usually branched, up to 2 feet tall.

Leaves Opposite, simple, ovate to ovate-lanceolate, without teeth, hairy, up to 3 inches long, with stalks.

Flower arrangement Several in branched, terminal clusters.

Flowers Up to 2 inches long, on slender stalks. **Sepals** 5, united at the base, hairy, green, the lobes narrow. **Petals** 5, funnel-shaped, lavender. **Stamens** 4, attached to the petals. **Pistil** Ovary superior.

Fruit Capsule oblong, finely hairy, up to 1 inch long.

Note There are four species of wild petunias (*Ruellia*) in Illinois. This is the first one to flower in spring. Al-

KEY FACTS

Perennial from thickened roots.

Habitat Moist to dry forests, glades, streambanks

Flowering late May to mid-autumn

though the flower does resemble the flower of a petunia, these plants are in different families.

BLUE STAR
Amsonia tabernaemontana Walt.

DOGBANE FAMILY | APOCYNACEAE

KEY FACTS

Perennial from thickened roots.

Habitat Woods, rocky ravines, seeps, streambanks, moist sandy meadows

Flowering mid-April to late June

Amsonia Named for Dr. Charles Amson, an 18th century Virginia physician and scientific explorer.

Flower arrangement Many in terminal clusters.

Flowers Up to ¾-inch across, on slender stalks. **Sepals** 5, narrow, united below, green, very small. **Petals** 5, united below in to a tube about as long as the lobes, pale blue. **Stamens** 5, attached near the top of the tube of the petals. **Pistil** Ovaries 2, superior, connected at the top by the style.

Fruit A pair of upright follicles up to 4 inches long, smooth.

Note This species does well in wildflower gardens.

Stems Upright, sometimes branched, smooth, up to 4 feet tall.

Leaves Opposite, simple, lanceolate to ovate-lanceolate, without teeth, smooth, up to 4 inches long, on short stalks.

WILD GINGER
Asarum canadense L.

Asarum Ancient Greek name.

Stems Aboveground stems absent.

Leaves Usually 2, opposite, borne near the ground level, broadly ovate, heart-shaped, up to 6 inches long, hairy, on long, hairy stalks.

Flower arrangement Solitary from the axil of the leaves.

Flowers Up to 1 inch across, on slender stalks. **Sepals** 3, united below, maroon-purple, the lobes triangular, pointed downward at the tip. **Petals** None. **Stamens** 12, attached to the ovary. **Pistil** Ovary inferior.

Fruit Capsule spherical, up to ⅓-inch in diameter, with the withered stamens and sepals attached to the top.

Use The aromatic rhizome can be used as a substitute for ginger.

KEY FACTS

Perennial herb from a thickened rhizome and fleshy roots.

Habitat Moist to somewhat dry woodlands, ravines

Flowering April and May

HOUND'S TONGUE

Cynoglossum virginianum L.

BORAGE FAMILY | BORAGINACEAE

KEY FACTS

Perennial from thickened roots.

Habitat Open rocky woods, streambanks, pastures, ravines

Flowering late April to late May

Synonym *Andersonglossum virginianaum* (L.) J.I. Cohen

Other name WILD COMFREY.

Stems Upright, rough-hairy, up to 2½ feet tall.

Leaves Basal and alternate, oval to

Cynoglossum Greek, *cynos*, of a dog, and *glossa*, tongue, in allusion to the shape and rough surface of the leaves.

oblong, without teeth, rough-hairy, the basal leaves up to 1 foot long and on stalks, the stem-leaves smaller and without stalks.

Flower arrangement Several in elongated, terminal clusters.

Flowers Up to ½-inch across, on hairy stalks. **Sepals** 5, united below, hairy, the lobes narrow. **Petals** 5, united below, blue. **Stamens** 5, attached to the petals. **Pistil** Ovary deeply 4-lobed, superior.

Fruit 4 nutlets, each about ⅓-inch long, covered with short, hooked barbs.

WATERLEAF
Hydrophyllum appendiculatum Michx.

Hydrophyllum Greek, *hydor*, water, and *phyllon*, leaf, the original species having very watery stems and petioles.

Stems Upright, sometimes branched, hairy, up to 1 foot tall.

Leaves Basal and alternate, palmately lobed into 5 or 7 shallow lobes, coarsely toothed, hairy, usually mottled with pale green and gray.

Flower arrangement Several in a terminal cluster.

Flowers Up to ½-inch across, on slender, hairy stalks. **Sepals** 5, attached at the base, lanceolate, green, hairy, with a tiny flap reflexed between each lobe at the base. **Petals** 5, united below, purple or violet. **Stamens** 5, attached to the petals. **Pistil** Ovary superior, styles 2.

Fruit Capsule spherical, up to 1/6-inch in diameter.

KEY FACTS
Perennial from tufts of roots.
Habitat Bottomland and mesic forests, base of bluffs
Flowering mid-April to mid-June

BLUEBELLS

Mertensia virginica (L.) Pers. ex Link

KEY FACTS

Perennial from a woody, somewhat rhizomatous rootstock.

Habitat Bottomland and mesic woods, streambanks

Flowering late March to late May

Other name VIRGINIA COWSLIP.

Stems Upright, sometimes branched, smooth, to 2 feet tall.

Leaves Alternate, simple, oblong to oval, smooth, without teeth, to 6 inches long.

Flower arrangement Several in terminal clusters.

Mertensia For Franz Karl Mertens, 1764-1831, German botanist.

Flowers Trumpet-shaped, up to 1¼ inches long, on short, smooth stalks. **Sepals** United below, 5-lobed at the tip, green, smooth, up to ¼-inch long. **Petals** 5, united below into an elongated tube, blue. **Stamens** 5, attached to the tube of the petals. **Pistil** Ovary superior, 4-lobed; style 1.

Fruit A cluster of 4 wrinkled nutlets.

Note This is a choice plant for wildflower gardens. Before opening, the flower buds are usually pink.

HAIRY PHACELIA
Phacelia bipinnatifida Michx.

Phacelia From the Greek *phacelos*, a fascicle, in allusion to the cymes.

Stems Upright, branched, hairy, up to 1½ feet tall.

Leaves Alternate, pinnately divided into 3-7 lobes, the lobes usually toothed, hairy, mottled with gray.

Flower arrangement Several in terminal clusters.

Flowers Up to ⅔-inch across, on slender, hairy stalks. **Sepals** 5, narrow, united at the base, green, hairy. **Petals** 5, united below, blue to violet. **Stamens** 5, attached to the petals, the stalks hairy. **Pistil** Ovary superior, styles 2.

Fruit Capsule spherical, up to ¼-inch in diameter.

KEY FACTS

Biennial from a thickened root.

Habitat Streambanks, bottomland forests, ravines, base of bluffs

Flowering mid-April to mid-May

MIAMI-MIST
Phacelia purshii Buckl.

BORAGE FAMILY | BORAGINACEAE

KEY FACTS

Annual from slender roots.

Habitat Bottomland and mesic woods, streambanks, base of bluffs, prairies, pastures

Flowering mid-April to mid-May

Stems Upright, branched, hairy, to 15 inches tall.

Leaves Basal and alternate, up to 3 inches long, pinnately divided into 9-15 lobes or leaflets, hairy, the lowest leaves on long stalks.

Flower arrangement Several in 1-sided, terminal clusters.

Flowers Up to ½-inch across, on slender stalks. **Sepals** 5, united below, green, the lobes narrowly lanceolate. **Petals** 5, united below, blue, the lobes fringed. **Stamens** 5, attached to the petals. **Pistil** Ovary superior, styles 2.

Fruit Capsule ovoid, up to ¼-inch long, hairy.

SMALL PHACELIA

Phacelia ranunculacea (Nutt.) Constance

Stems Upright, branched, hairy, to 8 inches tall.

Leaves Alternate, deeply pinnately 3 to 7-lobed, the lobes rounded at the tip, hairy.

Flower arrangement 1–5 flowers in a terminal raceme.

Flowers Up to ¼-inch across, on slender stalks longer than the flower. **Sepals** 5, united at the base, green, the lobes very narrow, hairy. **Petals** 5, united below into a short tube, pale blue. **Stamens** 5, attached to the tube of the petals. **Pistil** Ovary superior, styles 2.

Fruit Capsule spherical, up to 1/6-inch in diameter, hairy.

KEY FACTS

Annual from fibrous roots.

Habitat Rich woods, bottomland forests, ravines, base of bluffs

Flowering mid-April to the first week in May

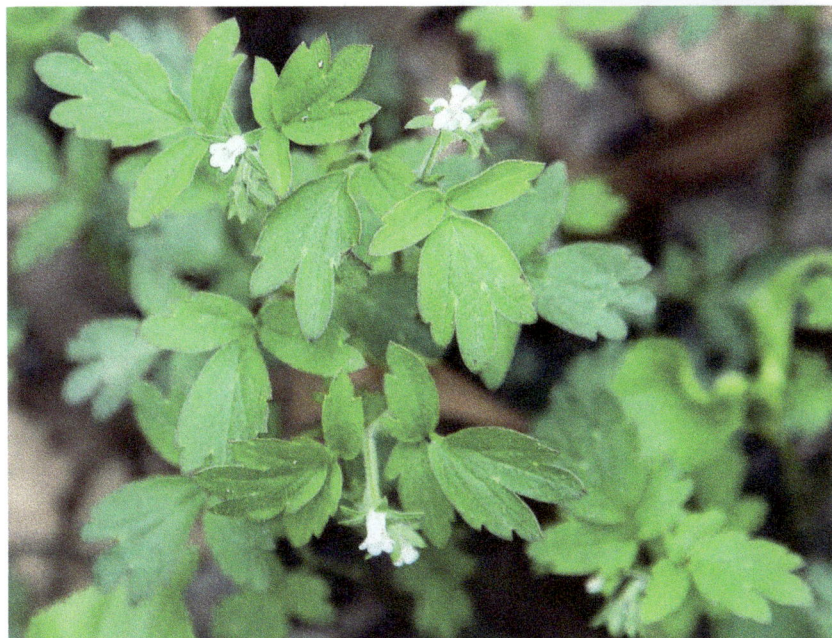

PURPLE CRESS
Cardamine douglassii Britt.

KEY FACTS

Perennial from a swollen base and with small tubers.

Habitat Mesic and bottomland woods

Flowering April

Cardamine Greek, *kardamon*, the name of some cress.

Flowers Up to nearly 1 inch broad, on stalks up to 1 inch long. **Sepals** 4, purplish. **Petals** 4, purple to lavender. **Stamens** 6. **Pistils** Ovary superior.

Fruit Pods upright, up to 1 inch long, about 1/12-inch broad, slender-tipped.

Use The young leaves may be used in salads.

Stems Upright, smooth or hairy, up to 1½ feet tall.

Leaves Basal leaves ovate to nearly round, angular-lobed, up to 1 inch broad, smooth or hairy, on long stalks; stem-leaves similar but usually coarsely toothed, on short stalks or without stalks.

Flower arrangement Several in a terminal raceme.

SMOOTH SPIDERWORT
Tradescantia ohiensis Raf.

Tradescantia For John Tradescant, gardener to Charles I of England.

Stems Upright, branched, smooth, often bluish, up to 3 feet tall.

Leaves Very elongated, up to 1½ feet long, up to ½-inch broad, smooth.

Flower arrangement Several in terminal umbels.

Flowers To nearly 2 inches across, on smooth stalks. **Sepals** 3, green, elliptic, smooth except sometimes for a tuft of hairs at the tip. **Petals** 3, blue. **Stamens** 6, with feathery stalks. **Pistils** Ovary superior.

Fruit Capsule up to ½-inch long, smooth, with several seeds.

KEY FACTS

Perennial from fleshy roots.

Habitat Upland forest openings, prairies, roadsides, fields, pastures

Flowering May to mid-summer

Note This common species is recognized by its bluish stems and general absence of hairs.

ZIGZAG SPIDERWORT

Tradescantia subaspera Ker-Gawl.

KEY FACTS

Perennial from fleshy roots.

Habitat Mesic and bottomland woods, ravines, shaded streambanks, often on calcium-rich soils

Flowering May until autumn

Flowers Up to 2 inches across, on hairy stalks. **Sepals** 3, green, broadly lanceolate, hairy. **Petals** 3, blue or purple, deteriorating quickly. **Stamens** 6, with feathery stalks. **Pistil** Ovary superior.

Fruit Capsule splitting open into 3 segments, with several seeds.

Use This is a handsome species for wildflower gardens.

Stems Upright, often pubescent, branched, up to 3 feet tall.

Leaves Elongate-lanceolate, sometimes more than 1 foot long, up to 2 inches broad, hairy.

Flower arrangement Several in terminal umbels.

VIRGINIA SPIDERWORT
Tradescantia virginiana L.

Stems Upright, more or less succulent, usually smooth, up to 2½ feet tall.

Leaves Very long and slender, up to 1 foot long, up to 1 inch broad, usually ciliate.

Flower arrangement 1–several in terminal umbels.

Flowers Up to 2 inches across, on rather short, smooth or hairy, stalks. **Sepals** 3, green, lanceolate, smooth or hairy. **Petals** 3, blue, purple, rose, or white, deteriorating quickly. **Stamens** 6, the stalks feathery. **Pistil** Ovary superior.

Fruit Capsule up to ½-inch long, splitting open into 3 segments, with not more than 12 seeds.

Use The leaves are said to be used in salads.

KEY FACTS

Perennial from fleshy roots.

Habitat Mesic to dry upland woods, bluff ledges, open rocky woods, glade edges

Flowering late April until early June

Note Most plants of this spiderwort are blue- or purple-flowered, although rose- or white-flowered forms occur in Illinois.

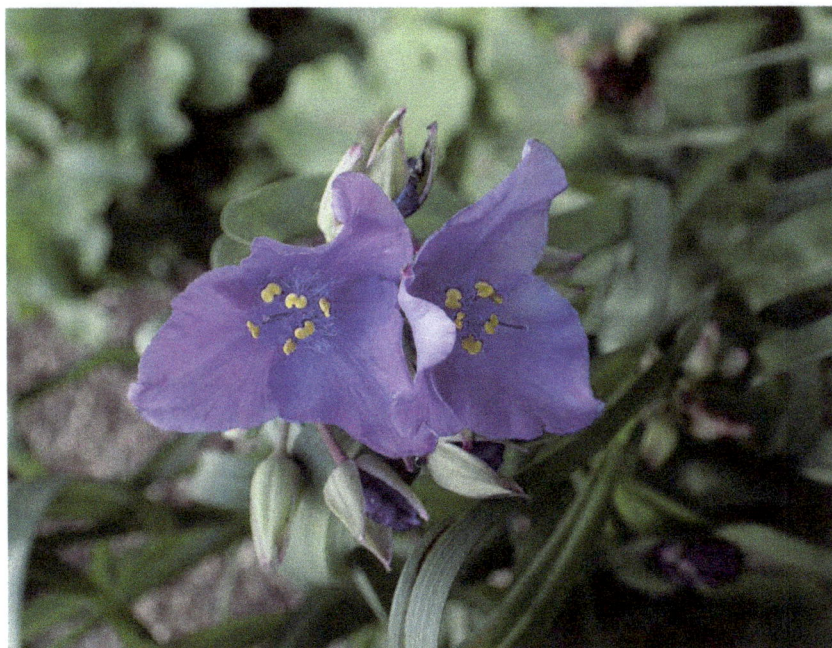

WILD GERANIUM
Geranium maculatum L.

KEY FACTS

Perennial from thickened rhizomes.

Habitat Bottomland and mesic forests, ravines

Flowering mid-April to late May

Stems Upright, sometimes branched, hairy, up to 1½ feet tall.
Leaves Basal leaves 3 to 5-lobed, hairy, to 5 inches broad, on long stalks; stem-leaves 2, opposite, smaller than the basal leaves, hairy, with a very short stalk.

Geranium Greek, *geranos*, crane; the long beak of the fruit was thought to resemble the beak of the crane.

Flower arrangement Few in a branched terminal cluster.
Flowers Up to 1½ inches broad, on hairy stalks. **Sepals** 5, green, awned at the tip. **Petals** 5, rose-purple, spotted, up to 1½ inches long, hairy at the base. **Stamens** 10, with 5 long and 5 short. **Pistil** Ovary superior, 5-parted, 5-beaked.
Fruit Capsules long-beaked, the beak up to 1½ inches long, splitting open from the top downward.
Use An attractive plant for wildflower gardens.
Note Although there are several other wild geraniums in the state, this is the only one found in woods.

BEE BALM
Monarda bradburiana Beck

Monarda Dedicated to Nicholas Monardes, 1493-1588, author of one of the first books on the plants of the New World.

Other names HORSEMINT, WILD BERGAMOT.

Stems Upright, usually unbranched, sometimes hairy, up to 1½ feet tall, square.

Leaves Opposite, simple, ovate to ovate-lanceolate, coarsely toothed, rounded at the base, hairy, without stalks.

Flower arrangement Several in a terminal head, subtended by green or purplish bracts.

Flowers Up to 1 inch long. **Sepals** 5, united below into a tube, the lobes tooth-like, green. **Petals** 5, pink, united below into a tube, forming an upper and lower lip, the upper

KEY FACTS

Perennial from thickened roots and rhizomes.

Habitat Rocky or dry open woods, fields, roadsides, soils often acidic

Flowering late April to late May

lip arched, the lower lip 3-lobed and purple-spotted. **Stamens** 2, attached to the petals. **Pistil** Ovary superior, 4-parted; styles 2.

Fruit A cluster of 4 smooth nutlets.

Use The leaves, aromatic and scented like oregano when crushed, can be made into a tea.

WILD SAGE
Salvia lyrata L.

KEY FACTS

Perennial from a short, thick rootstock.

Habitat Bottomland and mesic forests, streambanks, roadsides

Flowering late April to late May

Stems Upright, usually unbranched, hairy, to 2 feet tall.

Leaves Basal and opposite, hairy, the basal leaves pinnately lobed, up to 8 inches long, on long stalks; the stem-leaves smaller and few in

Salvia The Old Latin name.

number, pinnately lobed to merely toothed, without stalks.

Flower arrangement 6 flowers per cluster, with several clusters separated in a terminal spike.

Flowers Up to 1 inch long, on very short stalks. **Sepals** 5, united below, the lobes teeth-like but of different shapes, green. **Petals** 5, united into a slender tube below, the lobes arranged in 2 lips, the upper lip shorter than the lower, purple. **Stamens** 2, attached to the tube of the petals. **Pistil** 4-parted, superior; style 2-parted.

Fruit 4 nutlets in a cluster

Note In the Mint family, but these plants have little or no scent.

PURPLE TRILLIUM
Trillium recurvatum Beck

Trillium Latin, *tres*, three, in allusion to the regularly 3-parted flowers.

Other name PRAIRIE TRILLIUM, PURPLE WAKE ROBIN.

Stems Erect, unbranched, smooth, to 18 inches tall.

Leaves One whorl of 3, just beneath the flower, oval to ovate, pointed at the tip, rounded or tapering to the petiolate base, smooth, mottled, up to 4 inches long.

Flower arrangement Solitary.

Flowers Up to 1½ inches long, sessile. **Sepals** 3, green, reflexed, up to 1 inch long. **Petals** 3, maroon, erect, up to 1½ inches long. **Stamens** 6, shorter than the petals. **Pistil** Ovary superior, lobed; styles 3.

KEY FACTS

Perennial from short rhizomes.

Habitat Mesic and bottomland forests, ravines

Flowering late March to late May

Fruit An ovoid, 6-angled, dry berry up to ¾-inch long.

Use This trillium grows readily in a wildflower garden.

Note This is the only maroon-flowered *Trillium* in Illinois which has a sessile flower and stalked leaves.

SESSILE TRILLIUM

FALSE HELLEBORE FAMILY | MELANTHIACEAE

Trillium sessile L.

Flowers Up to 1½ inches long, sessile. **Sepals** 3, green, spreading, up to 1 inch long. **Petals** 3, maroon, ascending, up to 1½ inches long. **Stamens** 6, much shorter than the petals. **Pistil** Ovary superior, lobed; styles 3.

Fruit A nearly spherical, 6-angled, dry berry up to ½-inch in diameter.

Use Suitable for wildflower gardens.

Note There are 11 species of *Trillium* reported for Illinois, some of which are quite rare.

Other name SESSILE WAKE ROBIN.

Stems Erect, unbranched, smooth, to 10 inches tall.

Leaves One whorl of 3, just beneath the flower, oval to ovate, rounded or pointed at the tip, rounded at the base, smooth, usually mottled, up to 4 inches long, without stalks.

Flower arrangement Solitary.

ADAM-AND-EVE

Aplectrum hyemale (Muhl. ex Willd.) Torr.

Aplectrum *A–*, without, and *plectron*, spur.

Other name PUTTY ROOT.

Stems Leaf-bearing stems absent.

Leaf 1, basal, present from September to early May, then withering and gone by flowering time, elliptic to ovate, up to 6 inches long, up to half as broad, strongly veined.

Flower arrangement Several in terminal racemes, on a leafless stalk up to 1½ feet tall.

Flowers Up to 1 inch long, on short, smooth stalks. **Perianth** 6-parted, 5 of the parts narrowly lanceolate, yellow-brown and purple, up to ½-inch long, the sixth part, called the lip, 3-lobed, wavy-edged, less than ½-inch long. **Stamens and pistils** United into a central structure known as a column, curved, about ¼-inch long.

Fruit Capsule narrowly ovoid, nearly 1 inch long.

KEY FACTS

Perennial, usually from a pair of underground corms.

Habitat Rich, mesic woods

Flowering mid-May to early June

Note The single, corrugated leaf (below), after overwintering, withers prior to formation of the flowers.

SPRING CORALROOT
Corallorhiza wisteriana Conrad

ORCHID FAMILY | ORCHIDACEAE

KEY FACTS

Perennial from a coral-like rootstock.

Habitat Rich forests, soils often acidic

Flowering April

Corallorhiza Greek, *corallion*, coral, and *rhiza*, root, in allusion to the coralloid branches of the underground stem.

Flowers Up to 3 inches long, on short, ascending stalks. **Sepals** 3, narrow, greenish-yellow marked with purple-brown, 2 of them united at the base to form a spur. **Petals** 3, 2 of them narrow, greenish-yellow marked with purple-brown, the third, called the lip, broader, white with purple dots. **Stamens and pistils** United together to form a column, the column slightly winged at the base.

Fruit Capsule ellipsoid, drooping, less than ½-inch long.

Note Coralroot orchids do not have any green parts; they live as parasites on the roots of other plants.

Stems Upright, unbranched, purplish, up to 1 foot tall.

Leaves No green leaves present, but scale leaves are produced at the base of the stem and along the stem.

Flower arrangement Several in a terminal raceme.

SHOWY ORCHIS
Galearis spectabilis (L.) Raf.

Galearis From the Greek *galea*, helmet, referring to the helmet-like appearance of the flower.

Synonym *Orchis spectabilis* L.

Stems No leaf-bearing stems present.

Leaves 2, basal, obovate, smooth, up to 6 inches long and 3 inches broad, without teeth.

Flower arrangement Few, in a short, terminal spike.

Flowers Up to 1 inch long, purple and white, each subtended by a green leaf-life bract. **Sepals** 3, united to form a hood over the rest of the flower. **Petals** 3, more or less attached to the sepals, one of them projecting backward into a spur about 2/3 inch long. **Stamens and pistil** United into a central column,

KEY FACTS

Perennial from a cluster of fleshy roots.

Habitat Mesic or bottomland forests, ravines, lower slopes

Flowering mid-April to the end of May

the column purplish.

Fruit Capsule broadly ellipsoid, up to 1 inch long.

Note The flowers are *resupinate,* so what looks like the top of the flower is actually the bottom (and vice versa).

TWAY-BLADE ORCHID

Liparis liliifolia (L.) L.C. Rich. ex Ker-Gawl.

Perennial from a corm and thickened roots.

Habitat Dry to mesic upland woods, streambanks, slopes; soils acidic

Flowering May to early June

Liparis Greek, *liparos*, shining, from the glossy leaves.

smooth, slender stalks. **Perianth** 6-parted, 5 of the parts similar, very narrow, mauve-purple, the sixth part, called the lip, obovate, mauve-purple, up to ½-inch long. **Stamens** and pistil United into a short, curved, central column. **Fruit** Capsule ellipsoid, up to ½-inch long.

Stems No leaf-bearing stems present. **Leaves** 2, basal, oval to ovate, up to 5 inches long, about half as broad, smooth. **Flower arrangement** Several in a terminal raceme on a leafless stalk up to 10 inches long. **Flowers** Up to 1 inch long, on

PURPLE OXALIS
Oxalis violacea L.

Other name **VIOLET WOOD SORREL**.

Stems Upright, slender, smooth, unbranched, up to 8 inches tall.

Leaves All from the base of the plant, on long stalks, divided into 3 leaflets, the leaflets with a notch at the tip, smooth, often purple, at least on the lower surface.

Flower arrangement 2–10, at the end of a leafless stalk which is longer than the leaf stalks.

Flowers Nearly 1 inch long. **Sepals** 5, green, rounded at the tip. **Petals** 5, rose-purple, rounded at the tip, much longer than the sepals. **Stamens** 10, united at their base. **Pistil** Ovary superior.

Fruit Ovoid, smooth capsule, less than ¼ inch long, with several flat, wrinkled seeds.

Use The sour leaves, used sparingly because of their oxalic acid, can be added to salads.

Note In addition to this rose-purple species, several yellow-flowered species of *Oxalis* occur in Illinois (see page 33).

KEY FACTS

Perennial from a small bulb.

Habitat Woods, fields, bluff tops

Flowering mid–April to late June

BLUE-EYED MARY
Collinsia verna Nutt.

KEY FACTS

Annual from a slender taproot.

Habitat Bottomland forests, streambanks, base of bluffs

Flowering late April to late May

Stems Upright, usually smooth, to 1 foot tall.

Leaves Opposite, simple, sometimes finely hairy, the lower ovate, toothed or entire, short-stalked, the middle and upper leaves narrower, toothed, without a stalk.

Collinsia For Zaccheus Collins, Philadelphia botanist, 1764-1831.

Flower arrangement Flowers produced in the axils of the upper leaves.

Flowers Up to 2/3-inch long, on slender stalks up to 1 inch long. **Sepals** 5, narrow, united at base, green, usually sparsely hairy. **Petals** 5, united below, one group of three blue, the other 2 white. **Stamens** 4, attached to the tube of the petals. **Pistil** Ovary superior.

Fruit Capsule spherical, up to ¼-inch in diameter.

Note An attractive wildflower for rich, moist, shaded areas.

CLEFT PHLOX
Phlox bifida Beck

Phlox Greek for flame.

Other name SAND PHLOX.

Stems Spreading, wiry, much branched, hairy, sometimes nearly 1 foot long.

Leaves Opposite, simple, very narrow, up to 2 inches long, less than ¼-inch broad, hairy, without teeth.

Flower arrangement 1-few from the axils of the upper leaves.

Flowers Up to 1½ inches across, on slender, hairy stalks up to 1 inch long. **Sepals** 5, narrow, united below, green, hairy. **Petals** 5, united below, the lobes notched at the tip, lavender to pale purple. **Stamens** 5, attached to the tube of the petals. **Pistil** Ovary superior, stigmas 3.

Fruit Capsule oblong, up to 1/6-inch long.

KEY FACTS

Perennial from woody, often branched rootstocks.

Habitat Rocky and dry open woods, glades, prairies, bluffs

Flowering late March to mid-May

Note This is the first phlox to bloom in Illinois; often planted as an ornamental.

BLUE PHLOX
Phlox divaricata L.

KEY FACTS

Perennial with slender rhizomes.

Habitat Forests, streambanks, base of bluffs, roadsides

Flowering mid-April to early June

Other Name SWEET WILLIAM.

Stems Creeping as well as upright, finely hairy, up to 1½ feet tall.

Leaves Opposite, simple, lanceolate to oblong to ovate, finely hairy, without teeth, up to 4 inches long.

Flower arrangement Several in terminal clusters.

Flowers Up to 1¼ inches across, on slender stalks. **Sepals** 5, very narrow, united below, green, hairy.

Petals 5, united below into a slender tube, the lobes sometimes notched at the tip, blue to blue-violet. **Stamens** 5, attached to the tube of the petals. **Pistil** Ovary superior, stigmas 3.

Fruit Capsule oblong, up to 1/6-inch long.

Note Sweet William, sometimes applied to this plant, is also used for at least three other species in Illinois.

HAIRY PHLOX
Phlox pilosa L.

Stems Upright, very hairy, sometimes branched, up to 1¾ feet tall.

Leaves Opposite, simple, very narrow to lanceolate, hairy, without teeth, up to 4 inches long.

Flower arrangement Several in terminal clusters.

Flowers Up to 1¼ inches across, on slender, hairy stalks. **Sepals** 5, very narrow, united below, green, hairy. **Petals** 5, united below into a slender tube, the lobes not notched at the tip, pink to light purple. **Stamens** 5, attached to the tube of the petals.

Pistil Ovary superior, stigmas 3.

Fruit Capsule oblong, up to 1/6-inch long.

KEY FACTS

Perennial with taproot and slender rhizomes.

Habitat Woods, savannas, streambanks, fields, roadsides

Flowering late April through June

Use Easily grown from seed for the wildflower garden.

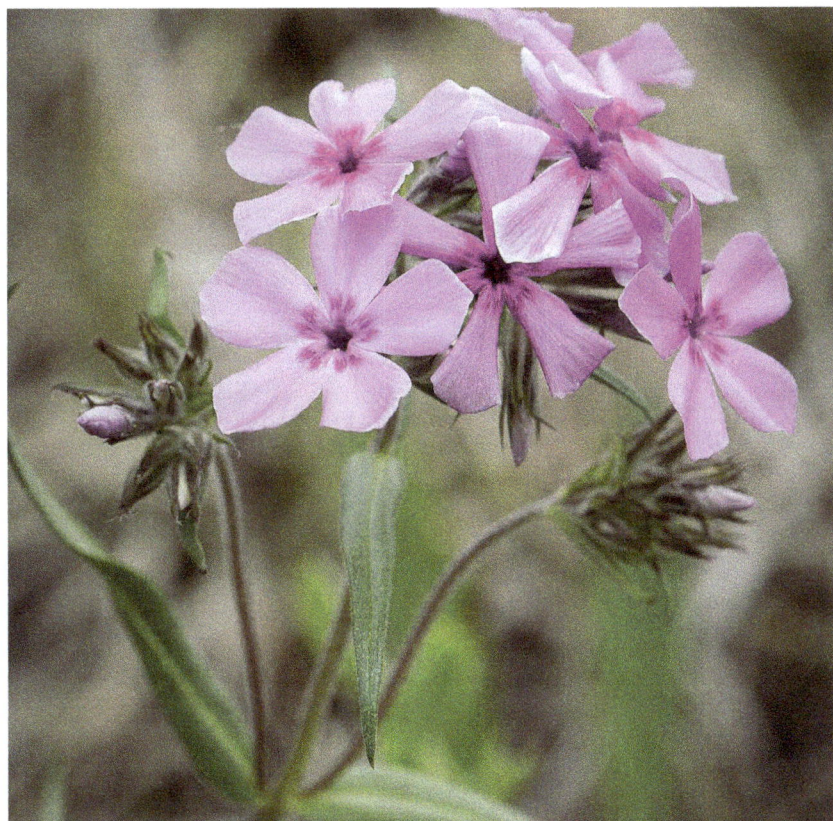

JACOB'S LADDER
Polemonium reptans L.

KEY FACTS

Perennial from a short woody rootstock and rhizomes.

Habitat Bottomland and mesic forests, , base of bluffs, streambanks

Flowering April and May

Other name GREEK VALERIAN.

Stems Upright or spreading, smooth, up to nearly 1 foot tall.

Leaves Alternate, pinnately compound, each leaf divided into 3-13 leaflets, the leaflets oblong, smooth, without teeth, up to 1¼ inches long.

Flower arrangement Several in a terminal cluster.

Flowers Up to ⅔-inch across, on slender, smooth stalks. **Sepals** 5, united below into a cup, green, smooth. **Petals** 5, united for about half their length, pale blue. **Stamens** 5, attached to the petals, not protruding from the flower. **Pistil** Ovary superior, stigmas 3.

Polemonium Ancient name.

Fruit Capsule ovoid, with usually 3 seeds.

Use This is an attractive plant for the wildflower garden. The plant has been used in herbal medicines for a variety of ailments.

Note Jacob's ladder is the only member of the Phlox family in Illinois which has compound leaves.

WILD LARKSPUR
Delphinium tricorne Michx.

Delphinium From *delphinus,* dolphin, in allusion to the shape of the flowers.

Other name DWARF LARKSPUR.

Stems Upright, smooth, unbranched, almost succulent, up to 2½ feet tall.

Leaves Basal and alternate, deeply palmately 5 to 7-lobed, smooth, the basal leaves on longer stalks.

Flower arrangement Several to many in a terminal raceme.

Flowers Up to 1½ inches long, stalked. **Sepals** 5, one of them developed into a spur up to 1 inch long. **Petals** 4, blue. **Stamens** Many.

KEY FACTS

Perennial from slender roots.

Habitat Rich woods

Flowering mid-April to late May

Pistils Usually 3, the ovary superior.

Fruit A cluster of 3 follicles up to ½-inch long, short-beaked; seeds several, dark.

Use This plant makes a beautiful addition to a wildflower garden.

Note Sometimes white-flowered specimens are found.

WILD VERBENA

Glandularia canadensis (L.) Nutt.

KEY FACTS

Perennial form slender roots.

Habitat Rocky woods, prairies

Flowering late March and during most of the summer

Glandularia Having small glands.

Petals 5, united below into a tube, bright purple to pink-rose. **Stamens** 4, attached to the tube of the petals. **Pistil** Ovary superior, 4-lobed; style 2-cleft.

Fruit 4 one-seeded nutlets, each about ¼-inch long.

Use This is an excellent plant for the wildflower garden because of its long flowering period.

Synonym *Verbena canadensis* (L.) Britt.

Other Name SWEET WILLIAM.

Stems Sprawling to upright, hairy, branched, up to 1½ feet tall.

Leaves Opposite, simple, up to 3 inches long, pinnately lobed, with each lobe toothed, hairy.

Flower arrangement Several, usually in terminal spikes.

Flowers Up to ¾-inch across, usually without a stalk. **Sepals** United below, with 5 teeth above, hairy.

BLUE VIOLET
Viola cucullata Ait.

Viola The ancient name.

Other name MARSH BLUE VIOLET.

Stems Leaf-bearing stems absent.

Leaves Arising from the base on smooth stalks, the blades ovate, heart-shaped at the base, finely toothed along the edges, smooth, up to 3 inches across.

Flower arrangement Solitary.

Flowers Up to 2 inches across, in stalks longer than the leaf stalks. **Sepals** 5, green, narrow and pointed. **Petals** 5, blue to violet, with club-shaped hairs on the lateral petals, with one petal spurred behind. **Stamens** 5, with 2 of them protruding into the spurred petal. **Pistil** Ovary superior.

Fruit Green capsule with several brownish seeds.

KEY FACTS

Perennial from a thickened rootstock.

Habitat Moist woods, also in marshes

Flowering mid-April to early June

Use The leaves of this species reportedly have been used in soups.

Note Although this violet is similar in appearance to others in the state, it is distinguished by the small, club-shaped hairs on the lateral petals.

BIRD'S-FOOT VIOLET
Viola pedata L.

VIOLET FAMILY | VIOLACEAE

KEY FACTS

Perennial with fibrous roots and a short, erect rhizome.

Habitat Openings in rocky or dry forests, savannas, prairies, blufftops, fields

Flowering mid-April to early June

Stems Leaf-bearing stems absent.

Leaves 3-parted, with each part usually 3-divided again, smooth, up to 2 inches across.

Flower arrangement Solitary.

Flowers Up to 1½ inches broad, on smooth stalks as long as or longer than the leaf stalks. **Sepals** 5, green, narrow. **Petals** 5, all lilac-purple, or the upper 2 sometimes velvety dark violet, none of the petals with a beard of hairs within. **Stamens** 5, with conspicuous orange anthers. **Pistil** Ovary superior.

Fruit Capsule green, smooth, with several copper-colored seeds.

Use An ideal plant for rock gardens.

Note The leaf shape and the absence of bearded petals readily identify this attractive species.

WOOLLY BLUE VIOLET
Viola sororia Willd.

Stems Leaf-bearing stems absent.

Leaves Arising from the base on smooth or hairy stalks up to 6 inches long, the blades ovate, pointed or rounded at the tip, heart-shaped at the base, scallop-toothed along the margins, smooth or more often hairy on the surfaces, up to 4 inches across.

Flower arrangement Solitary.

Flowers Up to 2 inches across, on long smooth or hairy stalks arising from the base. **Sepals** 5, green, smooth or hairy, usually lanceolate. **Petals** 5, blue to violet, with a beard of hairs on some of them, with one petal spurred behind. **Stamens** 5, usually with orange anthers, with 2 of them protruding into the spurred petal. **Pistil** Ovary superior.

Fruit Green to purple capsule up to ½-inch long, with spherical, dark brown seeds.

Use This is an easily grown species in wildflower gardens.

Note This violet is very common throughout the state. The seeds are not produced from the large, blue flowers, but from seldom seen small, apetalous flowers.

KEY FACTS

Perennial with a prostrate to ascending rhizome.

Habitat Forests, streambanks, prairies, savannas, fields

Flowering March to June; sometimes sporadically again in October and November

FALSE GARLIC
Nothoscordum bivalve (L.) Britt.

KEY FACTS

Perennial from a small bulb.

Habitat Forest openings, glades, prairies, streambanks, fields

Flowering late March to mid-May, often again in September and October

Stems Leaf-bearing stems absent.

Leaves All basal, long and narrow, up to ¼-inch wide, smooth.

Flower arrangement Several in a terminal umbel at the tip of a leafless stem.

Nothoscordum From the Greek *nothos*, false, and *skordum*, garlic, referring to the plant's relationship to *Allium*, but lacking the characteristic flavor and odor.

Flowers Up to ½-inch long, on smooth, slender stalks. **Perianth** 6-parted, the sepals and petals not distinguishable, white, lanceolate. **Stamens** 6, shorter than the perianth. **Pistils** Ovary superior.

Fruit Capsules 3-lobed, obovoid, smooth, up to ¼-inch long.

Note This species is related to the onion, which it resembles, but it has no onion odor. Little is known of its use in cooking.

HARBINGER-OF-SPRING
Erigenia bulbosa (Michx.) Nutt.

Erigenia Greek, *erigeniea*, early born.

Other name PEPPER-AND-SALT.

Stems Leaf-bearing stems absent, but flowers borne on a stalk which comes from the ground.

Leaves From base of plant, three times divided, with each division further divided into oblong, obtuse segments, smooth.

Flower arrangement Umbels of 1–4 rays.

Flowers Up to ¼-inch across, on very short stalks. **Sepals** Cup-shaped, green, smooth, with very short teeth or no teeth at all. **Petals** Five, white, ⅛-inch long. **Stamens** Five, as long as the petals, with dark purple anthers. **Pistil** Ovary inferior, 2-parted, with 2 recurved styles.

KEY FACTS

Perennial from deep tubers.

Habitat Rich shaded woods, alluvial soils along streams

Flowering Usually the first wildflower to bloom, beginning as early as first week in February

Fruit Nearly spherical, notched at each end, smooth, about 1/8-inch in diameter.

Note The dark anthers and white petals give the plant a "pepper and salt" appearance.

SWEET CICELY

Osmorhiza claytonii (Michx.) C.B. Clarke

KEY FACTS

Perennial from somewhat tuberous-thickened roots.

Habitat Mesic and bottomland forests, ravines, streambanks

Flowering mid-April to June

Other name WILD LICORICE.

Stems Upright, branched, white-hairy, up to 2½ feet tall.

Leaves Compound, 3-divided, with each division further divided into 5-9 toothed leaflets, hairy, the lowest leaves on longer stalks than the upper leaves.

Osmorhiza Greek, *osme*, scent, and *rhiza*, root.

Flower arrangement Many flowers in a 3- to 6-rayed umbel.

Flowers Small, on individual stalks about ½-inch long. **Sepals** Very small, with 5 tiny teeth, or the teeth absent. **Petals** 5, white, curved at the tip. **Stamens** 5, short. **Pistil** Ovary inferior, 2-lobed; style very short, not longer than the petals.

Fruit Fruit elongated, narrow, up to ½-inch long, hairy.

Use The roots, which contain anise oil, may be used as a seasoning.

Note This plant, when bruised, has a faint licorice aroma. A second species of rich woods, *Osmorhiza longistylis*, has the styles longer than the petals.

FALSE SOLOMON'S SEAL

Maianthemum racemosum (L.) Link

Maianthemum From Latin, *Maius*, May, and Greek *anthemon*, flower.

Synonym *Smilacina racemosa* (L.) Desf.

Stems Upright, unbranched, smooth or finely hairy, to 3 feet tall.

Leaves Alternate, lanceolate to oval, pointed at the tip, usually finely hairy on the lower surface, without teeth but often ciliate, up to 6 inches long and 3 inches wide.

Flower arrangement Several in a terminal panicle.

Flowers To 1/6-inch across, short-stalked. **Perianth** 6 segments, free from each other, not distinguishable into sepals and petals, white. **Stamens** 6, attached to the base of the perianth segments. **Pistils** Ovary superior, stigma 3-parted.

Fruit Berries red, spherical, up to ¼-inch in diameter.

Use Young stems may be prepared and eaten similar to asparagus. The berries act as a laxative if eaten in quantity.

KEY FACTS

Perennial with long-creeping rhizomes.

Habitat Mesic and bottomland forests

Flowering May to early June

STARRY FALSE SOLOMON'S SEAL

ASPARAGACEAE

Maianthemum stellatum (L.) Link

KEY FACTS

Perennial from thickened rhizomes.

Habitat Rich woods

Flowering mid-May to early June

Synonym *Smilacina stellata* (L.) Desf.

Stems Upright, smooth, unbranched, to 1½ feet tall.

Leaves Alternate, lanceolate, pointed at the tip, finely hairy on the lower surface, without teeth, sometimes bluish, up to 5 inches long and 1½ inches wide.

Flower arrangement Several in a terminal raceme.

Flowers Up to ¼-inch across, on slender stalks. **Perianth** 6 segments, free from each other, not distinguishable into sepals and petals, white. **Stamens** 6, attached to the base of the perianth parts. **Pistils** Ovary superior, stigma 3-parted.

Fruit Berries green or black, spherical, less than ½-inch in diameter.

Use The young leaves and stems may be cooked and eaten as greens.

SOLOMON'S SEAL

Polygonatum biflorum (Walter) Elliott

Polygonatum Greek, *polys*, many, and *gonu*, knee, in reference to the numerous joints of the rootstock.

Synonym *Polygonatum commutatum* (Schult.) A. Dietr.

Stems Upright, smooth, unbranched, sometimes as much as 6 feet tall.

Leaves Alternate, lanceolate to ovate, pointed at the tip, narrowed at the base, without teeth, up to 6 inches long and 4 inches broad, smooth.

Flower arrangement 2–10, hanging from the axils of the leaves.

Flowers Up to ¾-inch long, on slender, smooth stalks. **Perianth** 6-parted, united into a cylindrical tube, white. **Stamens** 6, not protruding from the flower. **Pistils** Ovary superior.

Fruit Berries dark blue, spherical, up to ½-inch in diameter.

Use The starchy rhizomes have been used to make bread, while the young stems may be prepared in the same manner as asparagus.

KEY FACTS

Perennial from thickened, jointed rhizomes.

Habitat Mesic and bottomland forests, ravines, streambanks

Flowering May until mid-June

PUSSYTOES
Antennaria parlinii Fernald

KEY FACTS

Perennial from elongated roots.

Habitat Dry woods, prairies, open disturbed areas

Flowering mid-April to early June

Antennaria Name from fancied resemblance of the pappus of the staminate flowers to the antennae of insects.

Flower arrangement Many flowers borne in terminal heads, with pollen-bearing male flowers on different plants from the pistil-bearing female flowers.

Flowers Pollen-bearing flowers in low, rounded heads; pistil-bearing flowers in more elongated heads; all heads with a series of narrow bracts at their base. **Sepals** None. **Petals** United into short tubular structure, white. **Stamens** 5, very small. **Pistil** Ovary inferior, surrounded by many silvery hairs; style 2-parted.

Stems Some creeping along the ground, some upright and up to 12 inches tall, all of them with mats of white, cobwebby hairs.

Leaves Basal leaves broadly oval to spatulate, strongly veined, with cobwebby hairs on the lower surface, to 3 inches long and 1½ inches broad; stem-leaves much narrower, densely hairy.

Fruit Achenes oblong, with a persistent tuft of white hairs at the tip.

Note This pussytoes can be distinguished from another common species, *Antennaria neglecta*, by its basal leaves and typical habitat. *A. neglecta* has basal leaves that are single-veined and more narrow, and isusually found in open habitats rather than woodlands.

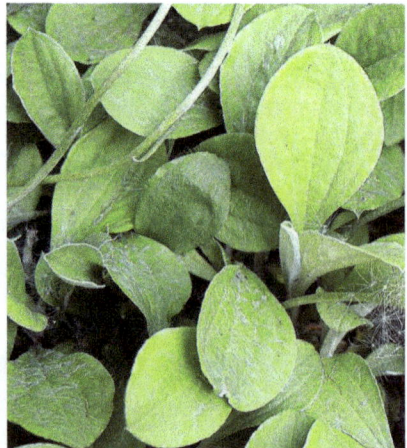

DAISY FLEABANE
Erigeron philadelphicus L.

Erigeron Greek *eri*, early, and *geron*, old man, in allusion to the pappus, which quickly becomes gray.

Stems Upright, usually hairy, branched, up to 3 feet tall.

Leaves Basal and alternate, hairy, the lower leaves spatulate to obovate, toothed, up to 3 inches long, the upper ones lanceolate, without teeth, much smaller.

Flower arrangement Many in a head, with several heads in terminal clusters, each head subtended by green bracts.

Flowers Two kinds, one of them white or pink and forming 100 or more rays, the other yellow and forming a central disk. **Sepals** None. **Petals** Either ray-like and white or short-tubular and yellow. **Stamens** 5. **Pistil** Ovary inferior, surrounded by silky hairs.

KEY FACTS

Biennial or perennial with fibrous roots.

Habitat Bottomland and mesic forests, streambanks, fields, savannas, prairies

Flowering April to early June

Fruit Achenes hairy, with a tuft of silky hairs at the top.

Use This plant has reputed medicinal properties. Native Americans used the plant as a cold remedy, analgesic, antidiarrheal agent, and a poultice for sores, and to reduce excessive bleeding following childbirth.

ROBIN'S PLANTAIN
Erigeron pulchellus Michx.

KEY FACTS

Perennial with fibrous roots and long, slender rhizomes or stolons.

Habitat Rocky open woods, thickets, streambanks

Flowering late April to early June

Stems Upright, unbranched, hairy, to 2 feet tall.

Leaves Basal and alternate, the basal spatulate to obovate, somewhat toothed, hairy, up to 3 inches long, the stem-leaves lanceolate to oblong, usually without teeth, hairy.

Flower arrangement Many flowers in a head, with a few heads in a terminal cluster.

Flowers Two types, one ray-like and white or violet, the other tubular, forming a central yellow disk. **Sepals** None. **Petals** Some united to form rays, others united to form short tubular flowers. **Stamens** 5. **Pistil** Ovary inferior, surrounded by white hairs.

Fruit Achenes smooth, with a tuft of hairs at the top.

Note May form colonies from its creeping stolons.

MAYAPPLE
Podophyllum peltatum L.

Podophyllum Greek, *podos*, foot, and *phyllon*, leaf.

Stems Upright, up to 2 feet tall, smooth.

Leaves Deeply 5- to 9-lobed, umbrella-like, usually smooth, up to 14 inches broad, attached at its center to the stalk.

Flower arrangement Solitary from the axils of a pair of leaves.

Flowers Up to 2 inches broad, nodding, on a stout stalk. **Sepals** 6, petal-like, shorter than the petals. **Petals** Usually 6, sometimes more, cream. **Stamens** Usually 12. **Pistil** Ovary superior.

Fruit Ovoid berry, yellow, smooth, up to 2 inches long.

Use The rhizome of this plant is poisonous and should be avoided. The fruit, however, is reported to be edible and may be eaten (sparingly) raw, even though they may be mildly toxic; the flavor is bland and similar to an overripe melon.

KEY FACTS

Perennial with long, creeping, branched rhizomes.

Habitat Mesic forests

Flowering late March to mid-May

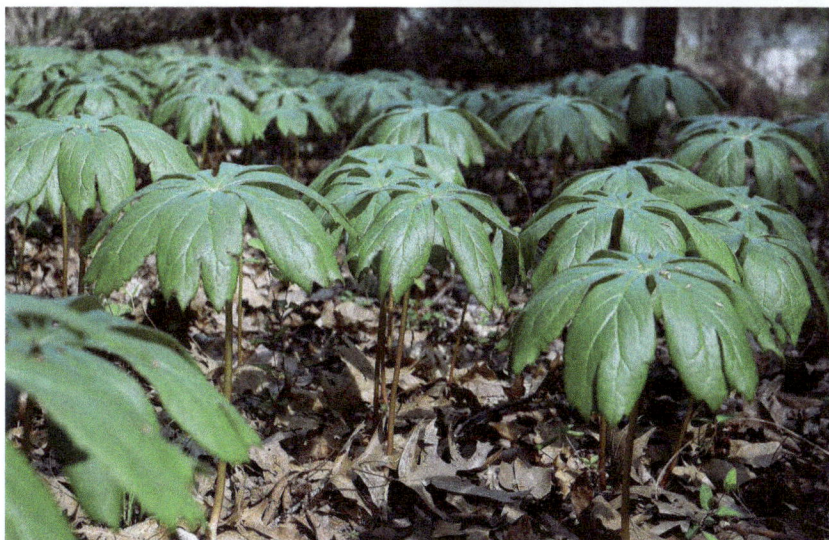

WILD FORGET-ME-NOT
Myosotis verna Nutt.

KEY FACTS

Annual from slender roots.

Habitat Woods, fields, prairies, glades, open, disturbed areas

Flowering mid–April to late May

Myosotis Greek, *myos*, of a mouse, and *ous,* ear, in allusion to the short and soft leaves in some species.

white. **Stamens** 5, attached to the tube of the petals. **Pistil** Ovary superior, 4-parted; style 1.

Fruit 4 one-seeded nutlets.

Note Although this plant has inconspicuous flowers, it is related to the familiar garden forget-me-not.

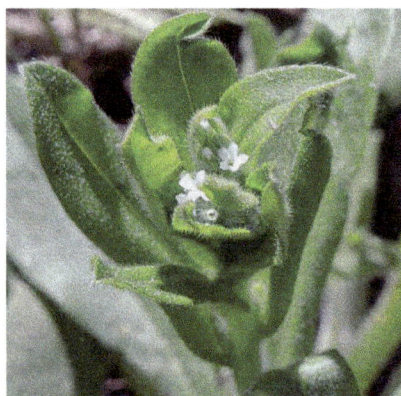

Other name SCORPION GRASS.

Stems Upright, branched, hairy, up to 1 foot tall.

Leaves Alternate, simple narrowly oblong, hairy, without teeth, up to 1 inch long.

Flower arrangement Several in curved, 1-sided, terminal racemes.

Flowers Up to ¼-inch across, on a short stalk. **Sepals** 5, united below, green, hairy. **Petals** 5, united below,

ROCK CRESS

Boechera laevigata (Muhl. ex Willd.) Al-Shehbaz

Boechera named after Danish botanist Tyge Böcher (1909–1983).

Synonyms *Arabis laevigata* (Muhl.) Poir., *Borodinia laevigata* (Muhl. ex Willd.) P.J. Alexander & Windham

Stems Upright, smooth, usually bluish and waxy, mostly un-branched, to 2½ feet tall.

Leaves Basal leaves spatulate, taper-ing to a stalk, coarsely toothed, smooth, to 3 inches long, persistent during the winter; stem-leaves al-ternate, entire, lanceolate, pointed at the tip, sagittate at the base, smooth, without stalks, not over-wintering.

Flower arrangement Several in a ter-minal raceme.

Flowers Up to ¼-inch long, slender, on slender stalks longer than the flower. **Sepals** 4, green, about half as long as the petals. **Petals** 4, white, about ¼-inch long. **Stamens** 6, usu-

KEY FACTS

Biennial from slender roots.

Habitat Rocky woods, bluffs, soils often cal-cium-rich

Flowering Usu-ally second week in April to first week in June

ally not protruding above the petals. **Pistil** Ovary superior, elon-gated; style nearly absent.

Fruit Capsule very slender, re-curved, up to 4 inches long but only about ½-inch broad, smooth, with winged seeds.

Note The overwintering basal leaves are often purplish.

BULBOUS CRESS

Cardamine bulbosa (Schreb. ex Muhl.) B.S.P.

KEY FACTS

Perennial from a swollen base, with short, tuberous rhizomes.

Habitat Wet woods, pond marrgins, sometimes in water

Flowering Last week in March to early June

Other name SPRING CRESS.

Stems Upright, often without branches, smooth, up to 18 inches tall.

Leaves Basal leaves oval to nearly round, smooth, sometimes with teeth, to 1½ inches long, on long stalks; stem-leaves alternate, oblong, smooth, coarsely toothed or

Cardamine Greek, *kardamon*, the name of some cress.

without teeth, up to 2 inches long, without a stalk.

Flower arrangement Several in a terminal raceme.

Flowers About ½-inch across, on smooth stalks up to 1 inch long. **Sepals** 4, green. **Petals** 4, white, much longer than the sepals. **Stamens** 6. **Pistil** Ovary superior.

Fruit "Pods" elongated, flat, smooth, erect, up to 1 inch long, with the persistent style prominent; seeds several, oval.

Use Young stems and leaves may be used in salads, and have a sharp peppery taste similar to horseradish.

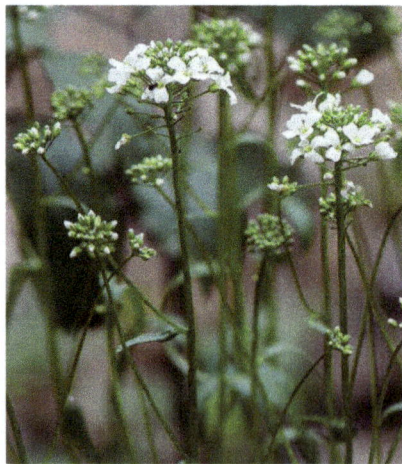

TOOTHWORT

Cardamine concatenata (Michx.) Sw.

Synonym *Dentaria laciniata* Muhl.

Other name Pepper-root.

Stems Erect, unbranched, smooth, up to 1 foot tall.

Leaves Very variable, 3 in a whorl below the flower, the rest basal, smooth, petiolate, palmately lobed, each lobe usually coarsely toothed.

Flower arrangement Terminal racemes.

Flowers Up to ¾-inch long and broad, slender-stalked. **Sepals** 4, green, about half as long as the petals. **Petals** 4, white or pale lavendar or pink, up to ½-inch long. **Stamens** 6, about as long as the petals.

Pistil Ovary superior, with a slender style.

Fruit Capsule-like, elongate and slender, smooth, up to 1½ inches long, with a single row of seeds.

KEY FACTS

Perennial from elongate rhizomes.

Habitat Low woods, moist slopes, ravines

Flowering early March to May

Use The fleshy rootstock tastes a little like a radish and can be used the same way a radish is used. When ground and mixed with vinegar, the rootstock has been used as a horseradish substitute.

BITTER CRESS

Cardamine pensylvanica Muhl. ex Willd.

KEY FACTS

Annual, biennial, or rarely short-lived perennial.

Habitat Moist to wet woods

Flowering mid-March to early summer

Other name BITTER CRESS.

Stems Upright, usually rather weak, smooth, branched, to 2 feet tall, usually shorter.

Leaves Alternate, pinnately compound, divided into 9–17 leaflets, the leaflets smooth, the terminal one oval, toothed, much larger than the narrow, often toothless, lateral ones.

Flower arrangement Clustered at the tips of the branches.

Flowers Up to ¼-inch across. **Sepals** 4, green, about half as long as the petals. **Petals** 4, white, up to ¼-inch long, broadly rounded at the tip. **Stamens** 6, shorter than the petals. **Pistil** Ovary superior.

Fruit Straight, slender "pods" up to 1¼ inches long, with flat seeds.

Use Young leaves and stems may be added to salads, imparting a mildly peppery taste.

Note A very similar plant, the **sand bitter cress** (*Cardamine parviflora* L.), differs in that the terminal leaflet is no broader than the lateral leaflets.

VEINY SKULLCAP
Scutellaria nervosa Pursh

Scutellaria Latin, *scutella*, a dish, in allusion to the projection of the fruiting calyx.

Stems Upright, usually smooth, mostly unbranched, up to 1 foot tall.

Leaves Opposite, simple, usually smooth, ovate to lanceolate, coarsely toothed, some of them more or less heart-shaped at the base, the lower ones on stalks, the upper ones without stalks.

Flower arrangement Few in the axils of the upper leaves.

Flowers Less than ½-inch long, on short stalks. **Sepals** 5, united into a structure which resembles a small bonnet, green. **Petals** 5, united below, white or pale blue, the lobes arranged into 2 lips, the upper lip arching, the lower lip 3-lobed. **Stamens** 4, attached to the tube of the petals. **Pistil** Ovary 4-parted, superior.

Fruit 4 slightly winged nutlets, borne on a short stalk.

KEY FACTS

Perennial from a thickened root and from slender, horizontal stolons.

Habitat Rich woods

Flowering late April to late May

SYNANDRA
Synandra hispidula (Michx.) Britt.

KEY FACTS

Biennial from thickened roots.

Habitat Uncommon in rich woods, southern Illinois

Flowering late April to mid-May

Stems Upright, hairy, to 2½ feet tall.

Leaves Opposite, simple, ovate, hairy, the lower ones heart-shaped at the base and on long stalks, the upper rounded at the base, without stalks.

Synandra Greek, syn, *together*, and *aner (andr)*, man, in allusion to the cohering locules.

Flower arrangement Solitary in the axils of the upper leaves.

Flowers Up to 1½ inches long, without stalks. **Sepals** 4, united below, green, the lobes as long as the tube, hairy. **Petals** 5, united below into a tube, showy, white, the lobes forming 2 lips, the lower lip 3-loped, purple-striped. **Stamens** 4, attached to the petals. **Pistil** Ovary 4-parted, superior; style 2-parted.

Fruit 4 nutlets, smooth.

Note Due to its rarity, listed as threatened by the state of Illinois.

NODDING TRILLIUM

Trillium flexipes Raf.

Trillium Latin, *tres*, three, in allusion to the regularly 3-parted flowers.

Other names WHITE TRILLIUM, WHITE WAKE ROBIN.

Stems Erect, unbranched, smooth, to nearly 2 feet tall.

Leaves One whorl of 3, just beneath the flower, very broad, pointed at the tip, up to 5 inches long, usually nearly as broad, smooth.

Flower arrangement Solitary.

Flowers Up to 3 inches across, on an arched, smooth stalk. **Sepals** 3, green. **Petals** 3, white, ovate. **Stamens** 6. **Pistil** Ovary superior, 6-lobed; stigmas 3, recurved.

Fruit Dry berry, angled, up to 1 inch in diameter.

Note This is the more common of the two large-flowered white trilliums in the state. It differs from *Trillium grandiflorum* by its recurved stigmas, but this is sometimes a dif-

KEY FACTS

Perennial with spreading rhizomes.

Habitat Rich bottomland forests, lower slopes of valleys and ravines

Flowering mid-April to late May

ficult characteristic to observe. Sometimes forming large colonies.

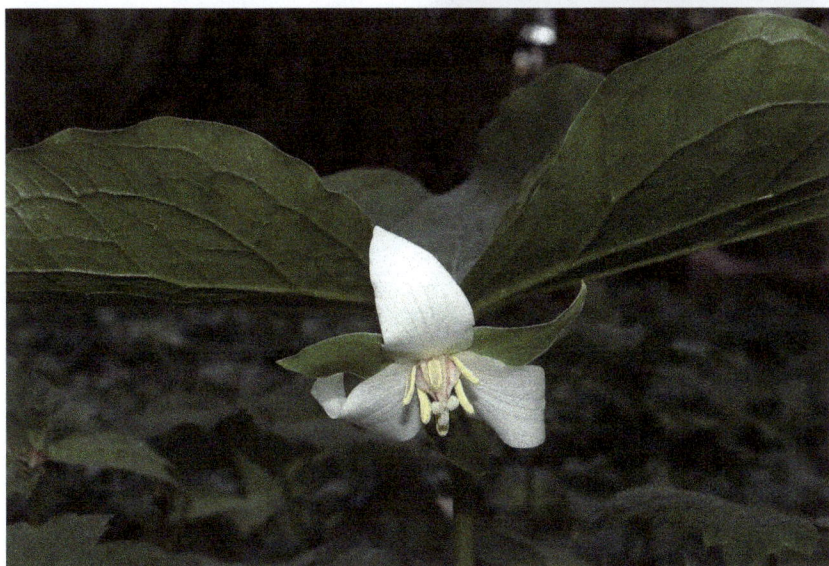

LARGE WHITE TRILLIUM FALSE HELLEBORE FAMILY | MELANTHIACEAE
Trillium grandiflorum (Michx.) Salisb.

KEY FACTS

Perennial from short, thickened rootstocks.

Habitat Rich deciduous woods, swamps, shaded riverbanks

Flowering May

smooth stalk. **Sepals** 3, green. **Petals** 3, white, sometimes pink, often obovate. **Stamens** 6. **Pistil** Ovary superior, 6-lobed; stigmas 3, erect. **Fruit** Dry berry, up to 1 inch wide.

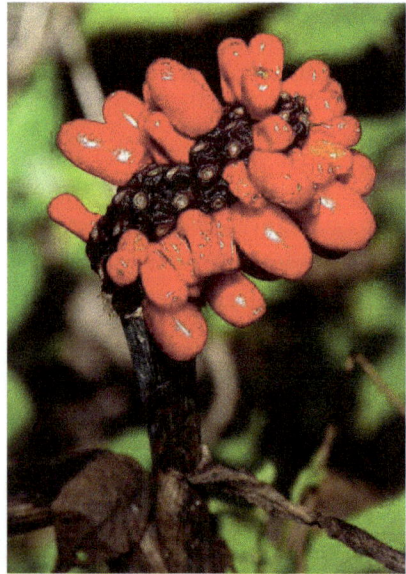

Other name LARGE WHITE WAKE ROBIN.

Stems Erect, unbranched, smooth, to 18 inches tall.

Leaves One whorl of 3, just beneath the flower, broadly ovate, pointed at the tip, up to 6 incles long, smooth.

Flower arrangement Solitary.

Flowers Up to 3 inches across, on an upright or somewhat curved,

SPRINGBEAUTY
Claytonia virginica L.

Claytonia Named for John Clayton, 1693-1773, one of the earliest American botanists.

Stems Upright, weak, smooth, to about 6 inches long.

Leaves Opposite, elongate and narrow, tapering to either end, without teeth, smooth, to 6 inches long, to ½-inch wide.

Flower arrangement Several in a terminal raceme.

Flowers Up to 1 inch across, on slender stalks. **Sepals** 2, green, smooth. **Petals** 5, veiny, white or pinkish, to ½-inch long, rounded to somewhat pointed at the tip. **Stamens** 5, with usually pink anthers. **Pistil** Ovary superior; style elongated, 3-parted.

Fruit Nearly spherical capsule, up to ¼-inch in diameter, with 3-6 flat seeds.

Use The tuberous roots may be boiled, salted, and eaten. They re-

KEY FACTS

Perennial from small, tuberous roots.

Habitat Rich moist woods, prairies, pastures

Flowering first week in March, may continue through May

putedly have the flavor of chestnuts. However, the tubers are small. Young leaves, rich in vitamins A and C, can be used in salads.

Note Springbeauty is probably the most common wildflower in Illinois. Some plants have broader leaves, but these are still the same species.

BROOMRAPE
Orobanche uniflora L.

KEY FACTS

Non-green annual, parasitic, growing on roots of other plants.

Habitat Rocky woods, prairies, glades

Flowering late April to early June

Synonym *Aphyllon uniflorum* (L.) Torr. & Gray

Other name ONE-FLOWERED CANCER-ROOT.

Stems Upright, hairy, up to 8 inches tall.

Leaves Reduced to narrowly ovate, non-green scales.

Flower arrangement Solitary at the tip of the stem.

Flowers Up to 1 inch long. **Sepals** 5, united below into a cup, hairy, the lobes tooth-like. **Petals** 5, united be-

Orobanche Greek, *orobos*, vetch, and *anchein*, to strangle.

low into an elongated, curved tube, white to lavender, hairy. **Stamens** 4, attached to the tube of the petals. **Pistil** Ovary superior.

Fruit Capsule ovoid, up to ½-inch long.

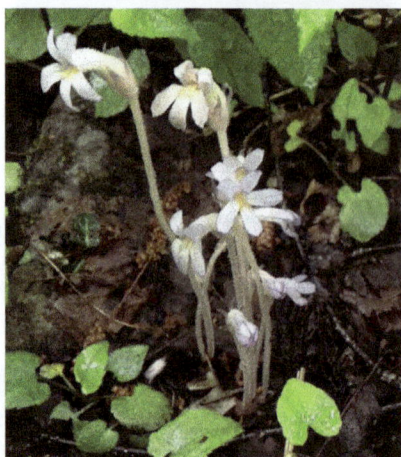

SQUIRREL CORN

Dicentra canadensis (Goldie) Walp.

Dicentra Greek, *dis*, twice, and *centron*, spur.

Other name TURKEY CORN.

Stems Leaf-bearing stems absent.

Leaves Basal, very delicately divided, smooth.

Flower arrangement Racemes on a leafless stalk up to 12 inches long.

Flowers Up to ⅔-inch long, up to ¾-inch broad, nodding, fragrant, on short stalks. **Sepals** 2, green, very small. **Petals** 4 in 2 pairs, white to yellowish-white, with rounded spurs at the base. **Stamens** 6, included within the petals. **Pistil** Ovary superior, stigma 2-parted.

Fruit Oblong to linear, smooth, splitting down 2 sides, to 1 inch long, with several seeds.

Use This plant contains an alkaloid poisonous to cattle.

KEY FACTS

Perennial from yellow, kernel-like tubers.

Habitat Rich moist woods, ravines

Flowering late March to mid-May

Note Distinguished from Dutchman's breeches by its yellow bulblets which resemble corn kernels (the bulblets of *D. cucullaria* are pink or white). The flowers of *Dicentra canadensis* also have rounded, slightly incurved petal spurs, unlike those of *D. cucullaria,* which are tapered and divergent.

DUTCHMAN'S BREECHES

Dicentra cucullaria (L.) Bernh.

POPPY FAMILY | PAPAVERACEAE

KEY FACTS

Perennial from pink to white grain-like bulblets.

Habitat Bottomland forests, ravines, along streams

Flowering mid- to late March to early May

Stems Leaf-bearing stems absent.

Leaves Basal, very delicately divided, pale beneath, smooth.

Flower arrangement Racemes on a leafless stalk up to 10 inches long.

Flowers Up to 2/3-inch long, up to ¾-inch broad, nodding, on short stalks. **Sepals** 2, green, very small. **Petals** 4 in 2 pairs, white except for the yellow tip, spreading above, with pointed spurs at the base. **Stamens** 6, included within the petals. **Pistil** Ovary superior, stigma 2-parted.

Fruit Oblong to linear, smooth, splitting down 2 sides, to 1 inch long, with several seeds.

Use The attractive leaves and flowers make this species popular in wildflower gardens. The plant contains an alkaloid poisonous to cattle.

Note This plant is closely related to squirrel corn, but usually blooms a little earlier.

BLOODROOT
Sanguinaria canadensis L.

Sanguinaria Name from the red color of the juice, from *sanguinarius*, bleeding.

Stems No aboveground leaf-bearing stems.

Leaves At base of plant, as broad as long, palmately lobed, heart-shaped at base, smooth, up to 3 inches across.

Flower arrangement Solitary on a leafless stalk.

Flowers Up to 1½ inches across. **Sepals** Two, green, falling as the flower opens. **Petals** 8–15, white, falling after a day, to nearly 1 inch long. **Stamens** Many and indefinite in number. **Pistil** Ovary superior, with one cavity; style very short.

Fruit Oblong capsule, abruptly tapered to each end, to 1 inch long, green, smooth, splitting along 2 sides. Each flower lasts only a very short time.

KEY FACTS

Perennial from a thick, horizontal, underground rhizome with red sap.

Habitat Rich, moist woods

Flowering By first of March. Each flower lasts only a very short time

Use The bitter rhizome, poisonous if swallowed in quantities, has been used medicinally as an emetic and purgative. The red sap in the rhizome was used by Native Americans as a face paint.

Note The leaf is usually inrolled around the flower stalk when the flower is open.

PALE BEARDTONGUE
Penstemon pallidus Small

PLANTAIN FAMILY | PLANTAGINACEAE

Penstemon From Latin, *pente*, five, and *stemon*, stamen; the 5th stamen being present and conspicuous, athough sterile.

lanceolate, without stalks.

Flower arrangement Several in an elongated, terminal cluster.

Flowers Up to 1 inch long, on short stalks. **Sepals** 5, united below, green, hairy, the lobes more or less triangular. **Petals** 5, united below into a tube, white or pale lavender. **Stamens** 5, attached to the petals, 1 of them not producing pollen but densely hairy. **Pistil** Ovary superior. **Fruit** Capsule ovoid, up to ¼-inch long.

Stems Upright, hairy, up to 2½ feet tall.

Leaves Basal and opposite, hairy, shallowly toothed, the basal oblong to elliptic, the upper oblong to

FRENCH'S SHOOTINGSTAR
Primula frenchii (Vasey) A.R. Mast & Reveal

Primula Prime, first, as in early blooming.

Synonym *Dodecatheon frenchii* (Vasey) Rydb.

Stems Leaf-bearing stems absent.

Leaves Basal, oval, abruptly contracted to a distinct stalk, smooth, entire or wavy-edged, up to 9 inches long and up to 4 inches broad.

Flower arrangement Few to several flowers in umbels at the tip of a leafless stalk.

Flowers Up to 1 inch long, on smooth stalks. **Sepals** 5, united below, green, pointed. **Petals** 5, white to lavender, turned backward, united at the base. **Stamens** 5, attached to the petals. **Pistil** Ovary superior, style slender.

KEY FACTS

Perennial from a thickened rootstock.

Habitat Under overhanging sandstone cliffs, uncommon in southern Illinois

Flowering mid-April to mid-May

Fruit Capsules ovoid to ellipsoid, ½-¾ inch long, splitting into 5 parts at the tip.

Note Sue to its rarity, this plant is listed as threatened by the state of Illinois.

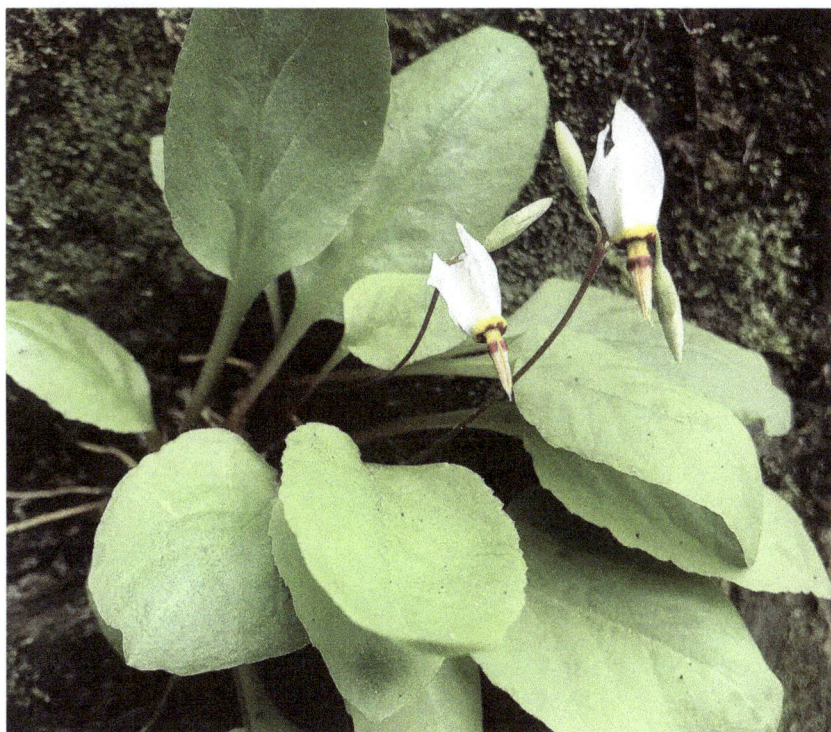

SHOOTINGSTAR

Primula meadia (L.) A.R. Mast & Reveal

KEY FACTS

Perennial with rhizomes.

Habitat Woods, prairies, glades, savannas, fields

Flowering mid-April to late May or early June

Synonym *Dodecatheon meadia* L.

Stems No leaf-bearing stem appears aboveground.

Leaves Basal, oblong to oblanceolate, tapering to the base, smooth, entire or wavy-edged, up to 1 foot long and up to 4 inches broad.

Flower arrangement Few to several flowers in umbels at the tip of a leafless stalk.

Flowers Up to 1⅓ inches long, on smooth stalks. **Sepals** 5, united below, green, pointed. **Petals** 5, white to lavender, turned backward, united at the base. **Stamens** 5, attached to the petals. **Pistil** Ovary superior, style slender.

Fruits: Capsules ovoid to ellipsoid, up to ¾-inch long, splitting into 5 parts at the tip.

Use This is a handsome species for wildflower gardens.

WHITE BANEBERRY
Actaea pachypoda Ell.

Actaea Ancient name for some plant.

Other name DOLL'S-EYES.

Stems Upright, branched, smooth or sometimes hairy, up to 2 feet tall.

Leaves Basal and alternate, doubly compound, the leaflets ovate, coarsely toothed, smooth or hairy.

Flower arrangement Several in terminal racemes.

Flowers Up to ¼-inch across, short-stalked. **Sepals** 3–5, white, falling away early. **Petals** 3-5 or more, white, very small. **Stamens** Numerous, white, giving the flower its basic color. **Pistil** Ovary superior, style absent.

Fruit Berries oval, shiny, white, marked with dark purple at one end.

Use The rhizome of this species has been used medicinally as a purgative. The berries are poisonuous.

KEY FACTS

Perennial from underground rhizomes.

Habitat Rich woods, ravines, north facing slopes

Flowering late April to late May

RED BANEBERRY

Actaea rubra (Ait.) Willd.

BUTTERCUP FAMILY | RANUNCULACEAE

KEY FACTS

Perennial from underground rhizomes.

Habitat Moist to mesic woodlands, shaded seeps and streambanks

Flowering May

Flowers Up to ¼-inch across, on stalks. **Sepals** 3–5, white, petal-like, falling away early. **Petals** Up to 10, white, shorter than the stamens. **Stamens** Many, white. **Pistil** Ovary superior.

Fruit Berries red, oval, up to ½-inch long.

Note Several parts of this plant, including the berries, are poisonous.

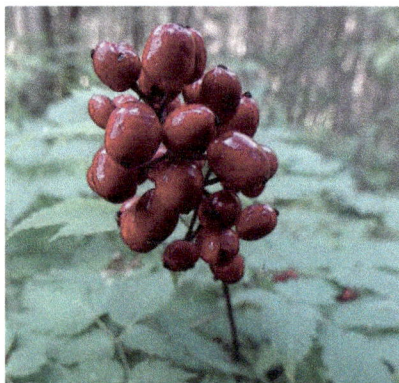

Other name RED DOLL'S-EYES.

Stems Upright, smooth or hairy, up to 2 feet tall.

Leaves Compound, divided twice into 3 divisions, the leaflets ovate, usually toothed, smooth or sometimes finely hairy.

Flower arrangement Several in terminal racemes.

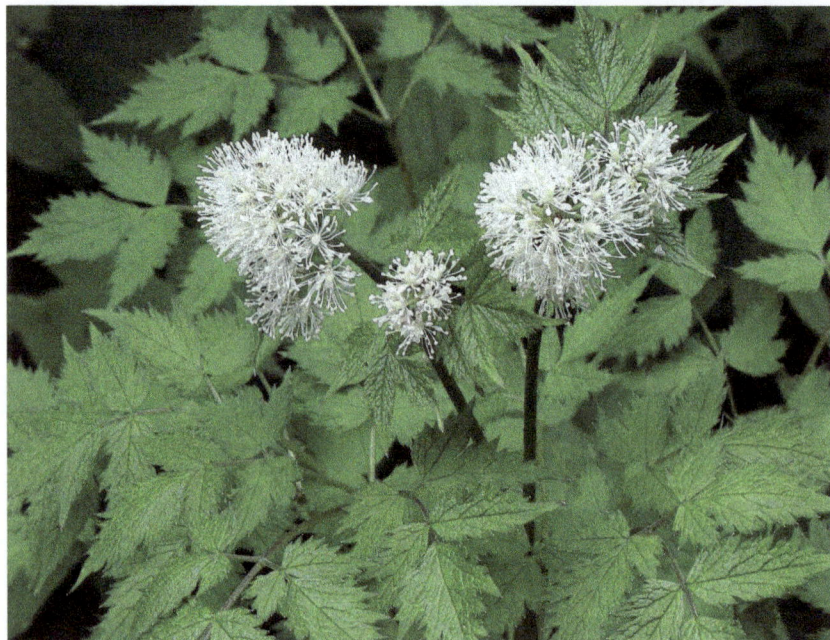

WINDFLOWER
Anemone quinquefolia L.

Anemone From the Greek, *anemos*, wind.

Stems Upright, smooth, un-branched, to 8 inches tall.

Leaves Basal leaves palmately 5-lobed, the lobes oblong, coarsely toothed, smooth, up to 2 inches long, long-stalked; stem-leaves 3 in a whorl near the top of the stem, each leaf palmately 3 or 5-lobed, the lobes oblong, coarsely toothed, smooth, shorter stalked.

Flower arrangement Solitary from the axils of the 3 stem-leaves.

Flowers Up to 1 inch across, on a slender stalk. **Sepals** 4-9, white to lavender, petal-like. **Petals** None. **Stamens** Many, surrounding the pistils, shorter than the sepals. **Pistils** Many in a central cluster, ovaries superior.

Fruit A central head of beaked achenes, each achene hairy.

KEY FACTS

Perennial from underground rhizomes.

Habitat Woods, mostly northern Illinois

Flowering late April to early June

RUE ANEMONE

BUTTERCUP FAMILY | RANUNCULACEAE

Anemonella thalictroides (L.) Spach

KEY FACTS

Perennial from several thickened roots.

Habitat Rocky woods, bluffs, glade margins

Flowering late March into June

Synonym *Thalictrum thalictroides* (L.) Eames & B. Boivin

Stems Upright, slender, smooth, unbranched, up to 8 inches tall.

Leaves Compound, divided into 3 divisions, with each part again divided into 3 leaflets, the leaflets oval, with 3 round, shallow lobes near the tip, smooth, the basal leaves on longer stalks.

Anemonella Diminutive of *Anemone.*

Flower arrangement Few in a terminal cluster.

Flowers Up to 1 inch across, on slender, smooth stalks. **Sepals** 5–9, white to pink to lavender, petal-like. **Petals** None. **Stamens** Many, surrounding the pistils. **Pistils** Several in a central cluster, the ovaries superior.

Fruit A cluster of achenes, each achene up to ½-inch long, pointed at the tip.

Use This is an attractive species for wildflower gardens.

Note This species is similar to the **false rue anemone** (page 107), but differs by having 3 whorled leaves just below the flower, with larger flowers often slightly tinted a pinkish color.

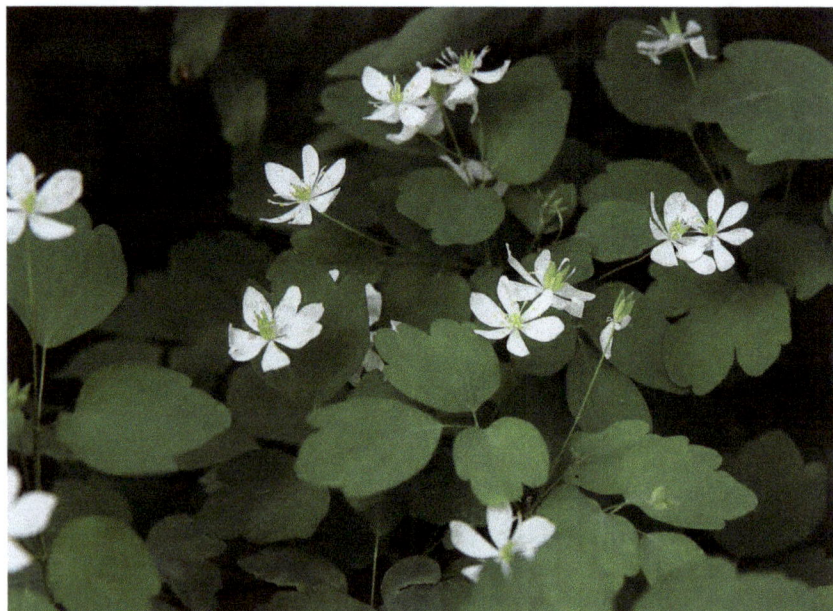

FALSE RUE ANEMONE
Enemion biternatum Raf.

Enemion From Greek, *enemion*, another word for anemone.

Synonym *Isopyrum biternatum* (Raf.) Torr. & Gray

Stems Erect, branched, slender, smooth, to 10 inches tall.

Leaves Twice 3-divided, with each leaflet 3-lobed, the lobes usually rounded at the tip, smooth, the lower leaves on long stalks, the upper leaves nearly stalkless.

Flower arrangement Several, in small, terminal clusters.

Flowers Up to ¾-inch across, on slender stalks. **Sepals** 5, petal-like, white to pinkish, veiny, less than ½-inch long. **Petals** None. **Stamens** Many. **Pistils** 2-10, with superior ovaries.

Fruit A cluster of ovate, spreading follicles, each up to ¼-inch long and

KEY FACTS

Perennial from fibrous roots, occasionally tuberous, and slender woody rhizomes.

Habitat Bottomland and mesic woods, streambanks, ravines

Flowering mid-March to early May

long-tapering to the tip, with several seeds.

Note Closely resembles **rue anemone** (*Anemonella thalictroides*), but that species has a set of whorled leaves just below the flowers, and is typically found in drier places.

HEPATICA

Hepatica nobilis Schreb. var. *acuta* (Pursh) Steyermark

KEY FACTS

Perennial from fibrous roots and rhizomes.

Habitat Forests, rock outcrops, soils usually calcium-rich

Flowering early March to early May

Synonym *Anemone americana* (DC.) H. Hara, *Hepatica acutiloba* DC.

Other name LIVERLEAF.

Stems No leaf-bearing stems present.

Leaves Basal, on long stalks, leathery, to 2½ inches broad, 3-lobed, veiny, each lobe tapering to a short point, hairy, more or less evergreen.

Flower arrangement Solitary, on long, hairy stalks to 8 inches tall.

Flowers Up to 1 inch across, subtended by 3, sepal-like bracts.
Sepals 5–9, petal-like, white to

Hepatica Latin, *hepaticus*, pertaining to the liver, alluding to the lobed leaves.

lavender, to ½-inch long. **Petals** None. **Stamens** Several to many. **Pistils** Several, with superior ovaries.

Fruit A cluster of several achenes, each achene up to 1/6-inch long, hairy, oblong, short-beaked.

Use This is a good species for a shaded wildflower garden.

Note The sepal color is variable, and ranges from pastel shades of blue or pink, to white. Plants with rounded-lobed leaves, in Illinois only found in the northeast corner, are known as var. *obtusa*. Its flowers are virtually identical.

GOLDENSEAL
Hydrastis canadensis L.

Hydrastis From resemblance to *Hydrophyllum canadense.*

Stems Upright, unbranched, hairy, up to 10 inches tall.

Leaves One leaf basal, palmately 5 to 9-lobed, highly textured when young, less so when mature, irregularly toothed, up to 8 inches across, hairy, on a long stalk; stem-leaves 2, at the tip of the stem, palmately 3 to 9-lobed, irregularly toothed, up to 6 inches across, hairy, on a short stalk.

Flower arrangement Solitary, arising from the base of the uppermost leaf.

Flowers Up to ½-inch across, on a short, hairy stalk. **Sepals** 3, whitish and petal-like, falling away early. **Petals** None. **Stamens** Numerous, white, giving the flower its color. **Pistils** Many in a central cluster, each with a superior ovary.

Fruit A head of closely grouped berries, each berry with 1 or 2 seeds and tipped with a short, curved beak.

KEY FACTS

Perennial with thick, yellow, creeping, usually branched rhizomes.

Habitat Bottomland and mesic forests, streambanks, ravines

Flowering mid-April to mid-May

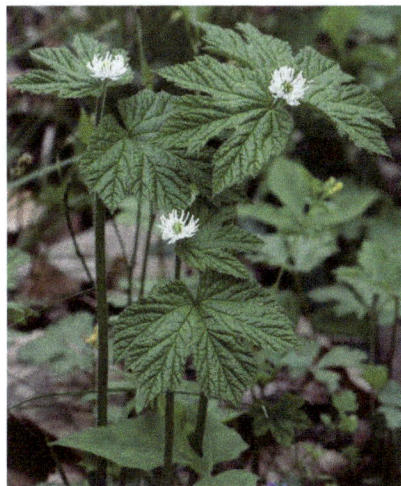

Use Similar to ginseng, the roots of this plant have reputed medicinal value, and have been heavily collected for its root.

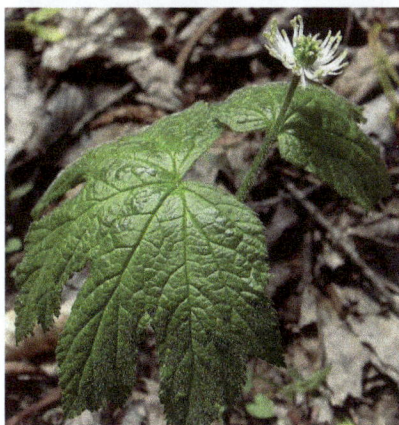

ROUGH BEDSTRAW
Galium aparine L.

MADDER FAMILY | RUBIACEAE

KEY FACTS

Annual from slender roots.

Habitat Forests, streambanks, marshes, ditches

Flowering late April to early June

Other Names GOOSE GRASS, CLEAVER, STICKY-WILLY.

Stems Sprawling, rough-hairy with downward pointing hairs, branched, up to 4 feet long.

Leaves 6 or 8 in a whorl, oblanceolate, short-pointed at the tip, rough hairy on the margins and on the mid-vein below, up to 3 inches long.

Galium Greek *gala*, milk; some species are said to cause curdling of milk.

Flower arrangement Few to several in clusters from the axils of the upper leaves.

Flowers Up to ¼-inch across, on stalks usually longer than the flowers. **Sepals** 4, united below, very tiny, green. **Petals** 4, united below, white. **Stamens** 4. **Pistil** Ovary inferior, styles 2.

Fruit Double, each part ellipsoid, up to ¼-inch long, covered with hooked bristles.

Use The seeds, when roasted, have been used as a substitute for coffee.

Note The bristles on the stems, leaves, and fruits enable this plant to adhere to clothing.

SMOOTH BEDSTRAW

Galium obtusum Bigelow

Other name BLUNT-LEAF BEDSTRAW.

Stems Spreading or sometimes upright, smooth, much branched to 15 inches long.

Leaves In whorls of 4, simple, narrowly lanceolate, up to 1 inch long, smooth, without teeth.

Flower arrangement Several in terminal clusters.

Flowers Up to 1/6-inch across, on slender stalks. **Sepals** 4, united for most of their length, green. **Petals** 4, united below, white. **Stamens** 4, attached to the petals. **Pistil** Ovary inferior, styles 2.

Fruit Double, dry, each part spherical, smooth, up to 1/6-inch long.

Note Identified by its moist to wet habitat, small white flowers, smooth stems and ovaries, and leaves which are usually 4 at each node.

KEY FACTS

Perennial from tufted roots.

Habitat Bottomland forests, swamps, marshes, streambanks, ditches

Flowering May and June

SUMMER BLUET
Houstonia longifolia Gaertn.

MADDER FAMILY | RUBIACEAE

KEY FACTS

Perennial from a tuft of fibrous roots.

Habitat Dry woods, savannas, upland prairies, glades

Flowering Last week in April to July

Houstonia For Dr. William Houston, 1695-1733, English botanist.

Flowers Up to ¼-inch long, on very slender, smooth stalks. **Sepals** 4, united below, the lobes narrow, green. **Petals** 4, united below into a tube, pale lavender or white. **Stamens** 4, attached to the petals. **Pistil** Ovary inferior.

Fruit Capsule spherical, 1/12-inch in diameter, subtended by the persistent sepals.

Note There are several different bluets in Illinois, and most of the pale-flowered ones are difficult to distinguish. Summer bluet is very similar in appearance to *Houstonia canadensis* (Canada Bluets); some authorities consider the latter species to be a variety of the former and name it *Houstonia longifolia* var. *ciliata*.

Stems Upright, slender, branched, smooth, up to 8 inches tall.

Leaves Basal and opposite, smooth, the basal leaves oval, up to ½-inch long, stalked, the stem-leaves very narrow, to 1 inch long, less than 1/6-inch broad.

Flower arrangement Several in branched, terminal clusters.

BISHOP'S-CAP
Mitella diphylla L.

Mitella Diminutive of *mitra*, cap, in allusion to the form of the young capsule.

Other name MITERWORT.

Stems Upright, hairy, bearing a pair of leaves some distance below the flowers, to 15 inches tall.

Leaves Most leaves basal, broadly ovate, heart-shaped at the base, shallowly 3 to 5-lobed, coarsely toothed, hairy, up to 2 inches long, on long stalks. One pair of nearly sessile leaves is midway on the stem, similar to the basal leaves but smaller and rounded at the base.

Flower arrangement Several along an elongated, terminal raceme.

Flowers Up to 1/3-inch across, on short stalks. **Sepals** 5-parted, green

KEY FACTS

Perennial from slender roots and with short, rhizomes.

Habitat Rich woods, often on wet rocks; base and ledges of cool slopes

Flowering early April to early May

below, the lobes white. **Petals** 5, cut like snowflakes, white. **Stamens** Usually 10, very short. **Pistil** Ovary superior, styles 2.

Fruit Capsule flat, splitting open at the upper end, with many shiny, smooth seeds.

WHITE VIOLET
Viola striata Ait.

VIOLET FAMILY | VIOLACEAE

KEY FACTS

Perennial with a prostrate to ascending rhizome.

Habitat Bottomland and mesic forests, streambanks, base of bluffs, prairies, glades, savannas

Flowering mid-April until near the end of May

Stems Several arising from the base of the plant, upright, smooth, angular, up to 10 inches tall, bearing jagged, leaf-like stipules where the leaves arise.

Leaves Alternate, nearly round to ovate, heart-shaped at the base, smooth, round-toothed along the edges, about 1½ inches long and broad, on long, smooth stalks.

Viola The ancient name.

Flower arrangement Solitary from the axils of the leaves, on long stalks.

Flowers Up to 1¼ inches long. **Sepals** 5, green. **Petals** 5, white, some with purple lines, one of them with a short, blunt spur. **Stamens** 5, free from each other. **Pistil** Ovary superior; style beaked, with some hair below the beak.

Fruit Ovoid capsule, smooth, up to ⅓-inch long, with pale brown seeds.

Use This is an attractive species for moist, shaded gardens.

Note In general, most of the blue violets in Illinois lack aboveground stems, while the white and yellow violets generally have aerial stems.

GREEN DRAGON

Arisaema dracontium (L.) Schott

Arisaema Greek *aris*, arum, and *haima*, blood.

Stems Leaf-bearing stems absent.

Leaf 1, from the base, divided into as many as 17 leaflets, the leaflets oblong, without teeth, smooth.

Flower arrangement Flowers crowded together at the base of a cylindrical column, called a **spadix**, which is prolonged into a tail-like, yellowish appendage up to 7 inches long. Spadix is surrounded by a protective green sheath.

Flowers Pollen-producing (male) flowers and pistil-producing (female) flowers sometimes borne on separate plants. **Sepals** None. **Petals** None. **Stamens** 4 per flower. **Pistil** Ovary superior.

Fruit Red-orange berries in thick heads.

KEY FACTS

Perennial from underground corms.

Habitat Bottomland and mesic forests

Flowering mid-April to late May

Use The corms cannot be eaten raw because of the presence of calcium oxalate crystals.

Note Identification is made easier by the distinctive leaves.

JACK-IN-THE-PULPIT

Arisaema triphyllum (L.) Schott

KEY FACTS

Perennial from underground corms.

Habitat Rich bottomlands, mesic forests, base of bluffs

Flowering April and May

Other name INDIAN TURNIP.

Stems No leaf-bearing stems present.

Leaf 1, basal, divided into 3 leaflets, the leaflets ovate to lanceolate, without teeth, smooth.

Flower arrangement Flowers crowded together at the base of a cylindrical column, called a **spadix**, overtopped by the arching **spathe**. The spathe may be green, purple, or purple-striped.

Flowers Very small, crowed together at the lower end of the spadix. **Sepals** None. **Petals** None. **Stamens** 4 per flower. **Pistil** Ovary superior.

Fruit Red berries in thick heads.

Use Dried corms were ground into flour by native tribes; they cannot be eaten raw as they contain oxalates, though they can be made edible by boiling

Note There is great variation in the color of the spathe.

SKUNK CABBAGE

Symplocarpus foetidus (L.) Salisb. ex Nutt.

Symplocarpus Greek, *symploce*, connection, and *carpos*, fruit, in allusion to the coalescence of the ovaries into a compound fruit.

Stems Leaf-bearing stems absent.

Leaves Several, basal, produced after flowering, smooth, without teeth, up to 2½ feet long and up to nearly 1 foot broad, with a stalk.

Flower arrangement Flowers crowded together on a thickened **spadix**, the spadix about 1 inch thick, surrounded partially by the **spathe**; the spathe purple-brown to greenish-yellow, up to 6 inches long, up to 3 inches broad.

Flowers Many crowded on a spadix. **Sepals** 4, small. **Petals** None. **Stamens** 4. **Pistil** Ovary more or less embedded in the spadix.

KEY FACTS

Perennial from thickened roots.

Habitat Shaded wet woods, swamps, seeps along wooded hillsides, springs

Flowering early March to early May

Fruit Berries sunken in the fleshy, enlarged spadix and attached to the persistent, fleshy sepals.

Use The roots, which contain starch, reputedly can be made into bread.

Note One of the very first wildflowers to bloom in the spring.

BLUE COHOSH

BARBERRY FAMILY | BERBERIDACEAE

Caulophyllum thalictroides (L.) Michx.

Caulophyllum Greek, *caulos*, stem and *phyllon*, leaf, alluding to the stem which seems to form a stalk for the large leaf.

on short stalks. **Sepals** 6, oblong, usually greenish, longer than the petals. **Petals** 6, greenish. **Stamens** 6. **Pistil** Ovary superior, style very short.

Fruit Fleshy "berries," ¼-⅓ inch in diameter, blue.

Use The fruit of the blue cohosh is said to be poisonous to eat and should be avoided.

Stems Upright, smooth, bluish and waxy, up to 3 feet tall, with a few leafless scales at the base.

Leaves Usually one leaf near the top of the stem and one near the bottom, each leaf 3-divided, the leaflets oval to oblong, coarsely toothed, smooth, 1–2½ inches long.

Flower arrangement Several to many in terminal clusters.

Flowers One-third to ½-inch across,

WOOD-RUSH
Luzula multiflora (Ehrh.) Lej.

Luzula From *Gramen Luzulae,* diminutive of *lux,* light, a name given from the shining of the plants with dew.

Stems Upright, unbranched, up to 15 inches tall.

Leaves Basal as well as on the stem, up to 4 inches long, less than ½-inch broad, hairy.

Flower arrangement Several in branched, terminal clusters. **Perianth** 6-parted, not distinguishable into sepals and petals, brown, pointed at the tip, up to 1/6-inch long. **Stamens** 6. **Pistils** Ovary superior.

Fruit Capsule usually obovoid, smooth, with 3 seeds.

Note Although not a showy flowering plant like most species in this book, wood-rush is included because it is common in many of the state's northern and southern woodlands.

KEY FACTS

Tufted perennial from fibrous roots, sometimes swollen at the base.

Habitat Upland woods, bluffs, shaded cliffs and ledges, sandy savannas, sand prairies

Flowering late March to early June

WOODLAND BLUEGRASS

Poa sylvestris Gray

GRASS FAMILY | POACEAE

KEY FACTS

Perennial from a tuft of roots.

Habitat Rich deciduous woods, wooded ravines, rocky wooded slopes

Flowering Last week in April to early June

Stems Upright, smooth, unbranched, up to 3 feet tall.

Leaves Up to 6 inches long, up to ¼-inch wide, rough to the touch on the upper surface, smooth on the lower surface.

Flower arrangement Many in a graceful, terminal panicle.

Poa Ancient Greek name for grass.

Flowers Arranged in green spikelets made up of 4 to 6 scales, all but the lowest two subtending stamens and pistils. The scales represent the perianth, which is absent. **Stamens** 3 **Pistil** Ovary superior, style plume-like.

Fruit Small grains.

Note Grasses are not covered in this book, except for the commonly encountered, spring-flowering woodland species *Poa sylvestris*.

HAIRY ALUMROOT
Heuchera americana L.

Heuchera For J. H. Heucher, German botanist, 1677-1747.

Stems Leaf-bearing stems absent.

Leaves All basal, broadly ovate to nearly round, up to 3½ inches across, with many spreading hairs, with 7–11 shallow, broad lobes.

Flower arrangement Many in an elongated cluster.

Flowers Less than ¼-inch long, on short, hairy stalks. **Sepals** 5, green, unequal in size, united below. **Petals** 5, purplish, spatulate, as long as or shorter than the sepals. **Stamens** 5, attached to the petals, protruding conspicuously from the flower, with yellow to orange anthers. **Pistil** Ovary more or less inferior, styles 2.

Fruit Capsule up to ¼-inch long, twin-beaked.

KEY FACTS

Perennial from thickened rootstocks.

Habitat Upland rocky woods and bluffs, wooded slopes; often found under oak trees

Flowering mid-April to early June

MARSH SAXIFRAGE

Micranthes pensylvanica (L.) Haw.

KEY FACTS

Perennial from tufted roots.

Habitat Wet, shaded sandstone ledges, ravines, lower slopes of rocky bluffs (usually north-facing)

Flowering late April to early May

Synonym *Saxifraga forbesii* Vasey

Stems Leaf-bearing stems absent.

Leaves Basal, broadly lanceolate to

Micranthes Greek *mikros*, small, and *anthos*, flower.

oval, very hairy, up to 10 inches long, up to 3 inches wide.

Flower arrangement Several in a terminal, rather narrow, cluster.

Flowers Less than ¼-inch across, on short, hairy stalks. **Sepals** 5, united at the base, usually turned downward. **Petals** 5, greenish, narrow, pointed, about twice as long as the sepals. **Stamens** 10. **Pistils** 2, united at base, each with a more or less inferior ovary and hooked style.

Fruit A pair of beaked follicles about ¼-inch long.

PELLITORY
Parietaria pensylvanica Muhl. ex Willd.

Parietaria The ancient Latin name.

Stems Upright or leaning, hairy, usually unbranched, up to 1 foot tall.

Leaves Alternate, simple, lanceolate, pointed at the tip, tapering to the base, hairy, without teeth, up to 3 inches long and ½-inch broad, on a short stalk.

Flower arrangement Several in a cluster from where the leaves arise.

Flowers Up to ¼-inch long, with usually 4 elongated green bracts easily mistaken for the sepals but longer than the sepals, some of the flowers only with stamens, others with both stamens and pistils.
Sepals 4, green, usually united below, ciliate. **Petals** None. **Stamens** 4.
Pistils Ovary superior, stigma appearing as a tuft of hairs.

Fruit Achene very tiny, at most about 1/20-inch long.

Note This is an obscure, often overlooked plant because of its inconspicuous flowers. It does not have the stinging hairs found in many nettles.

KEY FACTS

Annual from a small root, unarmed.

Habitat Rocky woods, glades, in dry soil under overhanging cliffs

Flowering May until early autumn

GREEN VIOLET

VIOLET FAMILY | VIOLACEAE

Hybanthus concolor (T.F. Forst.) Spreng.

KEY FACTS

Perennial herb from tufted roots and rhizomes.

Habitat Forests, glade margins, soils often calcium-rich

Flowering mid-April to early June

Synonyms *Cubelium concolor* (T.F. Forst.) Raf., *Viola concolor* T.F. Forst.

Stems Upright, hairy, unbranched, to 2 feet tall.

Leaves Alternate, simple, lanceolate, tapering to a point at the tip, usually without teeth, hairy, up to 4 inches long and up to 1¼ inches broad.

Flower arrangement 1-3 from the axils of the leaves.

Flowers Up to 1/3-inch long, on short, recurved stalks. **Sepals** 5, green, very narrow. **Petals** 5, greenish-white, one of them wider than

Hybanthus Greek, *hybos*, humpbacked, and *anthos*, flower, referring to the spurred lower petal.

the other 4 and swollen at the base. **Stamens** 5, the anthers adherent to the pistil. **Pistil** Ovary superior, style hooked.

Fruit Capsule 3-parted, oblongoid, up to 1 inch long, with several large, round seeds.

Note Although belonging to the Violet family, this plant looks nothing like other violets in Illinois.

Acaulescent. Lacking a stem, as for some plants like squirrel corn.

Achene. Small, one-seeded dry fruit, as in the sunflower family.

Acicular. Needlelike.

Acuminate. Tapering gradually to a point or apex as for leaf blades.

Acute. Terminating in a sharp point.

Alternate. Arrangement of leaves on the stem, with one leaf at each node.

Ament. Small inflorescence, usually a pendulous spike, with either male or female flowers, as in willows, or with only male flowers as in oaks, hickories, and several other tree genera; same as catkin.

Annual. Completing growth and reproduction in one season, after which the plant dies. A winter annual germinates in the fall and completes its cycle the following spring.

Attenuate. Tapering narrowly and gradually; a drawn-out tip.

Auricle. Minute appendage or lobe located at the summit of the sheath for some grasses and rushes.

Awl-shaped. Slender, sharp-pointed.

Awn. Slender bristle of various lengths.

Axil. Angle formed by the stem and the leaf (or between any two structures or organs).

Axis. Vertical or longitudinal portion, as for an inflorescence.

Berry. Soft or juicy fruit with several seeds.

Bipinnate. Doubly pinnate, with reference to compound twice-divided leaves.

Bract. Usually small foliaceous or awl-shaped organ subtending flowers or flower clusters; sometimes the reduced leaves on the upper stem of some plants.

Calyx. Outer whorl of mostly green parts below the petals of a flower.

Capitate. Headlike, usually dense, with reference to an inflorescence of numerous small individual flowers as in species of the sunflower flowers and various other plants.

Capsule. Many-seeded dry fruit which splits when ripened as in Jimson weed and many other plants.

Catkin. Same as ament.

Ciliate. With fringe of hairs on the margin.

Cleft. Cut or incised, like some leaf blades.

Compound leaf. A leaf with blade divided into several distinct leaflets.

Connate. United, joined together.

Cordate. Heart-shaped, referring to a leaf blade.

Corolla. The whorl of petals of a flower, separate or united.

Crenate. With rounded teeth on margin or base of leaf blade.

Crown. Branching portion of the tree or shrub; junction of stem and root in a herbaceous plant.

Culm. The stem of grasses or sedges.

Decreaser. A species that decreases in population density or cover with continuous overgrazing.

Decumbent. Prostrate or touching the ground, as applied to the stem.

Dehiscent. Splitting open at maturity.

Dentate. Toothed, as on the margin of the leaf blade.

Digitate. Fingerlike, referring to arrangement of spikes at the summit of a flower stalk, or to leaflets in some leaves.

Dioecious. Separate male and female flowers, each on different plants as in cottonwood.

Disk. The center part of a composite head, surrounded by ray flowers, or collectively referring to disk flowers as opposed to ray flowers.

Dissected. Cut or divided into narrow lobes, a leaf blade with deep incisions.

Downy. With soft fine hairs.

Drupe. Soft fruit with one stony pit, as in cherries and plums.

Elliptical. Widest at the middle and tapering similarly to both base and apex.

Entire. With no teeth or serrations on margins.

Exserted. Extending out of the sheath as a grass inflorescence.

Falcate. Curving to the tip, sickle-shaped.

Fascicle. Cluster, bundle.

Filiform. Threadlike.

Floret. The part of the spikelet comprising the lemma, palea, and flower.

Foliar. Referring to foliage or leaves.

Frond. Leaflike part of the fern plant.

Glabrous. Smooth, no hairs or roughness.

Glade. A dry, shallow soil area with sparse vegetation, and sometimes small trees and shrubs. Valuable for wildlife food and cover.

Glaucous. With a whitish bloom.

Glumes. Pair of empty (sterile) bracts or scales below the grass floret(s).

Habit. General shape of a plant.

Habitat. Natural location or site of a plant or animal, or of a community of plants and animals.

Hastate. Arrow-shaped.

Head. Dense cluster of flowers.

Herbaceous. Without perennial or woody stem.

Hirsute. With usually coarse hairs.

Hispid. With bristly hairs.

Incised. Deeply cut.

Increaser. A plant already present in an area which increases in abundance under overgrazing.

Inflorescence. Flowering stalk or cluster of flowers.

Internode. Section of the stem or culm between two successive nodes.

Involucre. Bracts surrounding a flower or flower cluster, as in sunflower.

Irregular. Unequal or dissimilar parts, with reference to the corolla of a flower.

Keeled. Sharply folded or with a dorsal ridge as a sheath.

Lacerate. With irregular indentations or cuts.

LANCEOLATE

OVATE

OBLONG

OBOVATE

SPATULATE

ELLIPTIC

LINEAR

ALTERNATE

OVAL

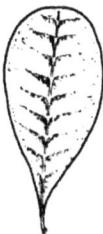
OBLANCEOLATE

SAGITTATE

OPPOSITE

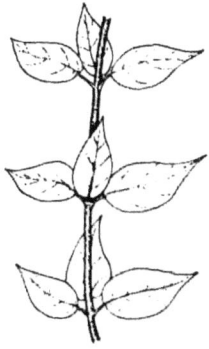
WHORLED

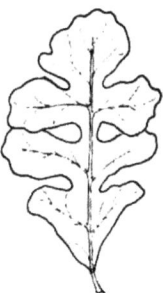
PINNATELY LOBED

PALMATELY LOBED

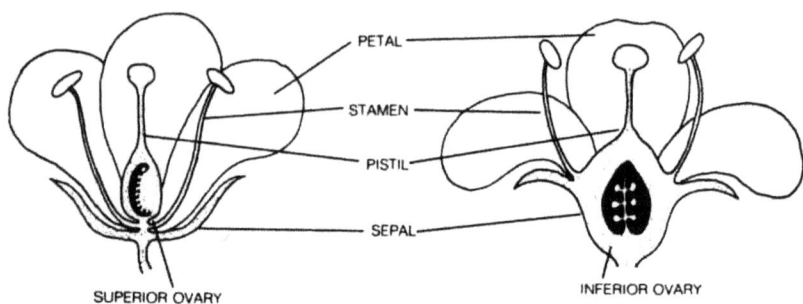

PETAL

STAMEN

PISTIL

SEPAL

SUPERIOR OVARY

INFERIOR OVARY

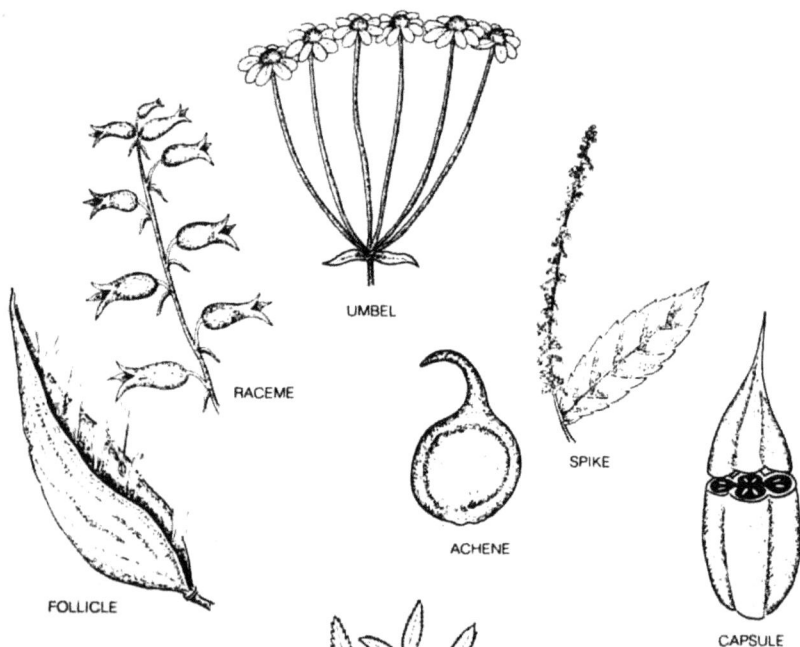

UMBEL

RACEME

SPIKE

FOLLICLE

ACHENE

CAPSULE

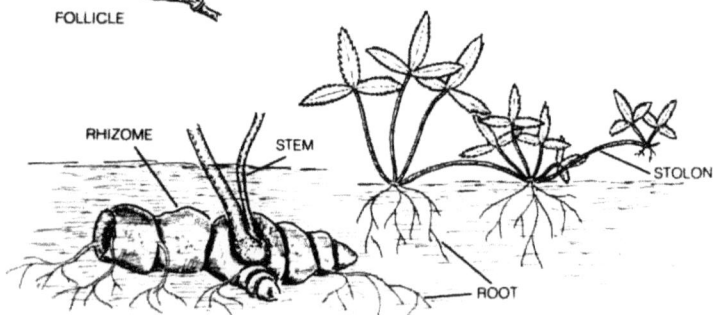

RHIZOME

STEM

STOLON

ROOT

Lanceolate. Usually elongate and tapering gradually to the apex.

Leaflet. Separate leaflike division of a compound leaf.

Legume. Pod, characteristic of the Pea family, splitting along both edges.

Lemma. One bract of the grass floret, opposite the palea.

Lenticel. Warty spots on bark of stems and branches as in elderberry, similar in function to stomata.

Ligule. Collarlike or hairy projection of grasses at the junction of the sheath and leaf blade; also used in reference to strap-shaped ray flowers in the Aster family.

Linear. Narrow, with parallel sides.

Lobe. Segment of a leaf rounded or angular at the apex, as for many oak leaves.

Loment. Special pod of the Pea family which breaks up into one-seeded parts as in the tick trefoils.

Lyrate. Broadest in the upper part of the leaf with a rounded apex, and incised and lobed toward narrowing base, as in bur oak.

Membranaceous. Thin, papery, or translucent.

Mebranous. Same as membranaceous.

Midrib. The main or central vein of a leaf.

Monoecious. Separate male and female flowers on the same plant as in oak, hazelnut, and hickory.

Node. Joint or location on stem from which leaves arise.

Obcordate. Inverted cordate, with broadest part toward the apex.

Oblanceolate. Inverted lanceolate, with broadest part toward the apex.

Oblique. Unequal or asymmetrical as for the base of leaf blade of elm.

Oblong. Longer than broad, with rounded apex and base.

Obovate. Inverted ovate, with broadest part toward the apex.

Obtuse. Blunt or wide-angled, as an apex of a leaf.

Opaque. Dark, not translucent.

Orbicular. Circular in outline.

Oval. Rounded-elliptic.

Ovary. Organ of the flower containing seeds.

Ovate. Egg-shaped in outline.

Palea. One bract of the grass floret, opposite the lemma and usually smaller than the latter.

Palmate. Lobes or veins arising from base of leaf blade.

Palmately compound. Leaflets all from summit of petiole or leaf stalk, as in buckeye.

Panicle. A type of compound inflorescence, much-branched, with stalked flowers or spikelets.

Papillose. Having hairs or projections with a swollen or glandlike base.

Parted. Deeply cut as in certain leaf blades, usually to the midrib.

Pedicel. Small stalk of a single flower or spikelet in a compound inflorescence.

Peduncle. Principal stalk of the inflorescence or head, also of a single flower where only one normally present.

Pendulous. Hanging down, limp.

Perennial. Plant persisting for several years.

Perfect flower. One with both male and female parts.

Perfoliate leaf. Stem passing through the blade of leaf.

Perianth. Whorls of the flower including calyx and corolla, or calyx only if petals absent.

Petiole. Stalk of leaf.

Petioled. With a petiole.

Pilose. With soft hairs.

Pinnate. Featherlike arrangement of veins, lobes, or leaflets along the midrib or main vein of leaf blade.

Pinnately compound. With leaflets of a compound leaf arranged along the rachis or central axis.

Pinnatifid. Lateral incisions or cuts toward the midrib of leaf blade.

Pistillate. Referring to the female flowers.

Pith. Spongy or central part of the stem or twig.

Prickle. Short sharp-tipped growth from surface bark or epidermis, as in blackberry.

Pubescent. With hairs.

Raceme. Simple unbranched inflorescence of stalked flowers or spikelets.

Rachis. Central axis of a compound leaf or flowering stalk.

Rays. Strap-shaped flowers around the central disk as in sunflower.

Regular. Equal and similar parts, with reference to petals of a flower.

Reniform. Broadly lobed at base with short blunt apex, as in some leaf blades; kidney-shaped.

Rhizome. Underground stem rooting at the nodes and producing new plants.

Rib. The main vein or veins of the leaf.

Root. Underground organ, lacking nodes.

Rootstock. Rhizome.

Rosette. Basal cluster of leaves.

Runner. Stolon.

Sagittate. Arrow-shaped, similar to hastate but basal lobes not spreading outward.

Scabrous. Rough-surfaced.

Scurfy. Mealy or scaly on the surface.

Segment. Lobes or parts of dissected leaf blade.

Serrate. Sawlike or sharp-toothed on the margin of the leaf, the teeth pointed toward apex.

Sessile. Lacking a stalk or petiole.

Sinus. The notch or space between lobes of a leaf.

Smooth. Glabrous, lacking pubescence; or leaf margins without indentations.

Spadix. The fleshy central floral structure bearing flowers as in Jack-in-the-pulpit.

Spatulate. Spoon-shaped; widest in the upper part, rounded at the apex and with long tapering base.

Spicate. Resembling a spike.

Spike. Simple unbranched inflorescence of sessile flowers or spikelets.

Spine. Sharp-pointed growth of variable length from the surface of branches or stem, as in roses or blackberry.

Sporadic. Scattered, erratic distribution.

Staminate. Referring to the male flowers.

Stellate. Star-shaped, as with starlike clusters of pubescence on a leaf blade.

Stigma. Upper part of the style that receives pollen.

Stipule. Bractlike appendage on each side of the base of the leaf petiole in certain plants.

Stolon. Prostrate or creeping runner rooting at nodes and producing new plants.

Tendril. Slender clasping stem or appendage, usually coiling.

Thorn. Sharp-pointed reduced woody branch.

Tomentose. Densely pubescent or woolly.

Truncate. Straight across, as if cut off.

Tuber. Thick or rounded underground stem with buds.

Umbel. A type of compound inflorescence, flat-topped or umbrella-shaped, pedicels arising from a common point.

Unisexual. Of single sex, either male or female.

Woolly. With densely matted hairs.

INDEX

Note Synonyms are listed in *italics*.